The Essential Vegan
Air Fryer Cookbook

THE ESSENTIAL *Vegan* AIR FRYER Cookbook

75 Whole Food Recipes to Fry, Bake, and Roast

Tess Challis

Photography by Marija Vidal

Foreword by JL Fields

ROCKRIDGE PRESS

Interior and Cover Designer: Amanda Kirk
Art Producer: Sara Feinstein
Editor: Bridget Fitzgerald
Production Editor: Ashley Polikoff
Photography © 2019 Marija Vidal. Food styling by Cregg Green. Author photo courtesy of © Melissa Schwartz
Cover recipe: Asian Buffet Bowl with Crisp Tofu, page 99

ISBN: Print 978-1-64152-413-1 | eBook 978-1-64152-414-8

*This book is dedicated
to you, dear reader.*

May it inspire you to create healthy,

delicious food at home that

nourishes you and those you love.

contents

FOREWORD . . . VIII
INTRODUCTION . . . X

chapter 1

Air Fryer Basics . . . 1

chapter 2

Breakfast & Breads . . . 17

chapter 3

Sides & Snacks . . . 43

chapter 4

Main Dishes . . . 73

chapter 5

Desserts . . . 107

chapter 6

Staples . . . 131

Air Fryer Vegan Food Chart . . . 144
The Dirty Dozen and the Clean Fifteen™ . . . 146
Measurement Conversions . . . 147
Recommendations and Resources . . . 148
Index . . . 150

FOREWORD

There's only one thing this cookbook author loves more than writing cookbooks. It's using the cookbooks written by my talented friends and colleagues. And this book you're holding? It's written by Tess Challis, the author of one of the first vegan books I ever bought: *Radiant Health, Inner Wealth*. She was my guide then and she continues to be to this day. Over the years we've bonded over all kinds of vegan professional connections—blogging, coaching, and teaching cooking classes—as well as our genuine love and passion for vegan cooking.

And that's where the air fryer, and this book, comes in. Four years ago I bought my first air fryer. Honestly, I thought it was kind of a hilarious concept. An "air" fryer? Who are these appliance makers fooling? But I bought one because a) I was seeing some pretty enticing air-fried creations online and b) I'm an appliance addict. I needed it. The air fryer was as magical as I had hoped. Dare I say more so? So magical that when I realized there were no vegan air-frying cookbooks out in the world, I needed to remedy that. A year later my book *The Vegan Air Fryer: The Healthier Way to Enjoy Deep-Fried Flavors* was published.

Since then, air fryers have become much more ubiquitous, even in vegan kitchens, and they aren't going anywhere anytime soon, as evidenced by the enormous number of brands now on the market and how much the appliance has evolved and improved. With those changes comes new ways in which we can cook with them. That's why four years later *this* cookbook lover and air-frying enthusiast is aching for updated and solid recipes for the clever appliance. Sure, you can find air fryer recipes with one quick Google search, but I think we all know that we can trust a seasoned vegan chef and author who has dedicated her career—her life—to making a recipe *just right* so that we can all experience incredible and easy plant-based cooking and eating.

Tess holds your hand through the process if you're new to air-frying, covering everything from how they work to why you want to use one to the variety of ways in which you can cook with them. Longtime air-frying fans will love Tess's answers to questions like "Why isn't my food cooking evenly?"—which is still asked by folks who've been doing this for years. (Hint: Move that food!) And everyone will enjoy the recipes because Tess provides methods and approaches reflecting the evolution of what we've learned about air-frying over the years. Originally everyone was simply trying to master some version of deep-fried, battered food. (And there's nothing wrong with that! I'm looking at you, Crunchy Onion Rings and Kids' Taquitos!) But the air fryer is so much more than a "fryer." You can bake, roast, and grill wholesome and often healthier versions of favorite foods like Pasta with Creamy Cauliflower Sauce, Simple Roasted Zucchini, and Roasted Shishito Peppers with Lime. Why use an air fryer instead of your oven or stove? Because you can create these delectable foods in a small kitchen without the mess and smell of greasy, hot oil, and during the long hot days of summer you can enjoy piping-hot favorites without overheating your home.

In person, Tess is super funny, very direct, and always wants you to succeed—and she has laid out a book that delivers on all three. I have had a blast cooking out of *The Essential Vegan Air Fryer Cookbook* and I think you will, too. Tess has your back!

Jl Fields

Master vegan lifestyle coach and educator, founder of the Colorado Springs Vegan Cooking Academy, and author of Vegan Meal Prep, The Vegan Air Fryer, *and* Vegan Pressure Cooking.

INTRODUCTION

You know that feeling when you discover something new that you absolutely love, and then later wonder how you ever lived without it? That's exactly how I feel about my air fryer—and what I'm hoping will happen for you as you enter the world of air-fried vegan recipes. I've made it my mission to offer you the most delicious, nutritious recipes possible, with easy-to-follow directions that anyone can master. Even if you're new to this fabulous appliance, you'll truly feel like a pro after cooking your way through this book. And if you're already comfortable with this appliance, that's great too—you'll have fun expanding your horizons to create crowd-pleasing masterpieces in your air fryer!

Because of my dedication to healthy living, this book prioritizes fresh, whole food ingredients. Even though I enjoy the occasional vegan cheese or plant-based meat (there's no need for perfection—balance is the key), my philosophy is that plant-based whole foods are ideal for optimal nutrition. And if this sounds at all limiting, you're about to be pleasantly surprised. Healthy vegan eating is truly about abundance—not deprivation. If you're new to vegan food, you're about to discover the versatility of plant-based eating.

In fact, back in 1991—in the first few months of being vegan—I was struggling, partly due to focusing on all the foods I "couldn't" have anymore. Then, I had an epiphany: I realized that when I focused on the new world of food I was discovering, there was actually more variety than ever before! Decades later, this is even more true. The "restriction" of eating a plant-based diet is purely mental. When you embrace vegan eating, a previously unknown world of flavorful, satisfying food reveals itself to you. Over the years, I've discovered Thai, Ethiopian, Indian, and other delicious cuisines that I'd never given the time of day before going vegan.

In this book, I share many of these cuisines, with the added bonus of being able to prepare them all in an air fryer. It's only been a few years since I started cooking with that little dynamo, but we've been inseparable ever since. It quickly became my most-used kitchen appliance because of its versatility, ease of use, convenience, and consistently great results.

Even if you've had bad luck with cookbooks before, I'm excited for you to give these recipes a whirl. They're tried and true—not only with my own successes, but also those of my dedicated testing group. This is what led me to writing cookbooks in the first place! In my early days of plant-based living, I found it incredibly frustrating (and expensive) to try new recipes only to be disappointed with the results. I vowed to one day create dependable cookbooks that would give excellent results and full flavors every time. This book aims to deliver on my promise.

When you combine solid vegan recipes and your new best friend, the air fryer, the variety and possibilities are endless. I hope you'll have as much fun air-frying up these recipes as I do, and I can't wait to see what you cook up!

chapter 1

Air Fryer Basics

In the chapter ahead, we'll dive into the basics, and get you all set up for air-frying success in your own kitchen. All you need are three things:

1. **An air fryer** (you saw that one coming, right?) and some basic accessories and pantry staples. I'll outline all of that for you before we get to the recipes.

2. **An appetite**—preferably for delicious vegan food.

3. **A can-do attitude.** Even if you haven't had luck in the kitchen before, it's a new day, and I believe in you! Like they say in the movie *Ratatouille*, "Anyone can cook!" Follow these recipes, and you'll be well on your way to surprising yourself—and impressing your friends and family.

THE ADVANTAGES OF THE VEGAN AIR FRYER

So, you're obviously intrigued by the idea of air-frying, or you wouldn't be reading this book right now. But you may also be wondering what all the fuss is about: Are air fryers really all that special? Should you give in and become one of those air fryer people? Absolutely! Come to the dark side with us. We have air-fried onion rings and lemon bars here.

In all seriousness, air-frying is a delicious way to shortcut traditional cooking and put a healthy spin on it. Here are some of the reasons I use the air fryer more than anything else in my kitchen:

❋ **It's healthy.** There's just no comparison between deep-frying and air-frying. When you air-fry your food, you reduce the fat content by up to 80 percent, making it heart-healthy and conducive to a healthy weight and better cholesterol profile.

❋ **It's oh-so-easy.** There's something great about being able to dump a bunch of food in a basket, walk away, and come back to delicious, crispy, cooked food.

❋ **It's faster than cooking in the oven.** I've found my air fryer cooks food almost twice as quickly as my oven. Saving time in the kitchen means more time, you know, eating.

❋ **Air-fried food is delicious!** It can give you the taste and texture of fried food, with loads of flavor—but without loads of fat. It's such a wonderful way to satisfy fried-food cravings in a healthier way.

❋ **The air fryer is ideal for vegan cuisine.** You can roast all manner of vegetables, make tofu a million different ways, bake potatoes, create delicious vegan snacks, and even whip up superb vegan desserts.

❋ **You'll spend less time cleaning up.** Oh, how I love this part! I remember life before my air fryer, when I'd have to scrub cookie sheets after I baked French fries or zucchini sticks. It's so much quicker to clean up an air fryer basket, and if you're used to frying your food in a pan or deep fryer, you'll also love not having to clean up oil spatters.

How It Works

People always ask, "How do air fryers work?" Sometimes I even get asked if it's just as unhealthy as frying in oil! Clearly, there's some confusion on the topic, so I'm here to simplify things. An air fryer is a small kitchen appliance that cooks your food by circulating hot air around it using the convection mechanism. Basically, it's a miniature super powered convection oven that crisps food with air instead of oil, letting you enjoy healthier versions of your favorite treats.

Although the air fryer cooks with, yes, air, you can still use oil in your device (and honestly, the food will taste better if you do). However, you'll definitely be using far less fat than you would if you were frying your food in the traditional manner. And even though you're using considerably less oil, your dishes will end up tasting fried and delicious. I mean, seriously—how great is that? In terms of cooking for your health, air-frying is essentially the same as baking and gives you a wide range of options—you can bake, fry, roast, and even make desserts in your air fryer.

CHOOSING A MAKE AND MODEL

The air fryer market is expanding so quickly. All kinds of brands are jumping on the air fryer bandwagon, offering their version of this appliance. In order to determine which air fryer model will make you the happiest, you'll want to weigh your options.

Factors to Consider

Air fryers vary in size, features, and the accessories they include. If you have a big family, you'll probably want to purchase a larger model to reduce the number of batches you'll have to make. On the other hand, if you're short on counter space, consider a standard 2- to 3-quart size. The air fryers that are 4 quarts (or larger) will require more space—about the same footprint as a toaster oven.

Some other things to consider are the temperature range and maximum allotted time for the preset timer. For example, the timer on some models may only go up to 30 minutes, which can be annoying if you're preparing a 40-minute recipe. Even worse, some air fryers don't have an adjustable temperature gauge, which means a lot of guesswork when making recipes that call for higher or lower temps. An air fryer with adjustable temperature settings is worth the extra price because it'll save you hassles in the end.

Some brands include accessories, which can seem like an enticing option. However, I personally don't use air fryer accessories—in fact, I purchased a round pan that doesn't typically go with air fryers because it has much higher sides than standard air fryer pans, which makes life so much easier. I recommend you opt for the best air fryer for you (without worrying about the accessories they include), and then purchase a good 6-inch pan (that's at least 2 inches deep), as we'll use that quite frequently in this book.

I personally use the GoWISE 3.7 quart air fryer, for several reasons. First of all, it's what I bought many years ago when I was on a tight budget (it's less than half the price of many other brands). Even with daily use over the years, it still works as well as it did when I first purchased it, and it's the perfect size for my small family. I like the simplicity of it too—it has no spinning parts that automatically stir (and sometimes break) food, and it's very intuitive and easy to use.

Fryers to Consider

MODEL	SIZE	PROGRAMMABLE BUTTONS	INCLUDED ACCESSORIES	TEMPERATURE RANGE	TIMER
PHILIPS XL	2.65 pounds	Yes	None	180 to 390°F	60 minutes
GoWISE	3.7 or 5.8 quarts	Yes	None	175 to 400°F	30 minutes
NUWAVE	3 or 6 quarts	Yes	Grill pan Baking pot Cupcake liners Carrying case	100 to 390°F	2 hours
POWER AIR FRYER	3.4 or 5.3 quarts	Yes	Baking insert Pizza pan Cooking tongs	180 to 400°F	60 minutes
T-FAL ACTIFRY	2.2 pounds	No	None	338°F (only one setting)	99 minutes

GET COOKING

By now, I hope you're getting excited about creating delicious masterpieces in your air fryer! To ensure success with the recipes I've created for you, please be sure to read through the tips that follow.

Step-by-Step Start

Are you an air fryer newbie? That's great! You've come to the right place. I'm here to simplify the process for you, and get you cooking like a pro in no time. Here are some basics to remember as you begin:

* **Read through the instruction manual, as all air fryers are different.** Also, wash the air fryer basket before your first use.

* **When removing food from your air fryer, remember that it's fine to remove the basket and turn it over to release your food, but never turn over the air fryer itself.**

* **Cut your food into consistent-size pieces, so they'll cook for a similar length of time.** For example, when making French fries, you don't want some pieces to be ¼-inch thick, and others to be ¾-inch thick, or the smaller pieces will be done before the larger ones.

* **Try not to layer food inside the basket.** You want the hot air to circulate freely around your food, so it can brown evenly. Keep your food in a single layer whenever possible, and cook the rest in subsequent batches.

* **Be sure to keep a neutral-flavored cooking oil spray on hand, and use it liberally when you want to create that delicious "fried" taste (see page 13 for more on oil).** You can purchase cooking oil spray from health food stores or supermarkets (I personally like the coconut oil spray from Trader Joe's).

* **I don't call for too many accessories, but you'll definitely want a 6-inch round baking pan (with sides that come up at least 2 inches).** Also grab a heat-proof rubber or silicone spatula.

* **Always set the timer on your air fryer, so you don't accidentally burn your food!** For the first few recipes you try, I recommend setting your timer for 1 to 2 minutes less than my recipes call for. That way, if your air fryer cooks more quickly than mine, you won't overcook your food.

Okay friends, here's where I get real with you. My top three tips for the air fryer involve a lot of practicality, with a good pinch of laziness. Because who doesn't want some shortcuts in the kitchen?

Tip One: You don't have to thoroughly clean your air fryer every single time you use it, especially if it's being used solely for vegan food. Since I use my air fryer multiple times a day, this one is a lifesaver. (I actually remember a squeal of delight from a cooking student when I mentioned this in class once, so I know I'm not the only lazy cook.) Most of the time, all you need to do is wipe your air fryer basket down with a clean cloth or paper towel, and then you can get on with your life. However, if you've made something very sticky in the basket, or just whipped up a batch of garlic potatoes (and you're about to make cinnamon crisps), you'll need to do a proper wash.

Tip Two: Oil spray wants to become your new best friend, and I strongly encourage you to accept that request. I suggest you keep a neutral-flavored oil spray (such as refined coconut, sunflower, or safflower) on hand at all times. And please don't be afraid to use enough of the spray to actually make your foods taste deliciously fried (and not dry).

Remember, you're making a much better choice by air-frying (vs. deep-frying) your food, so a few sprays of oil will still result in a healthy, low-fat dish.

Tip Three: Know thy appliance. Being a perfectionist, and wanting to give you absolutely tried-and-true recipes, I've carefully tested every recipe in this book, along with a wonderful group of recipe testers making the dishes in their own air fryers. We found that certain air fryers, like ovens, required slightly altered cooking times. Air fryers also vary in their temperature setting options, so if you don't have the exact temperature the recipe calls for, simply round down to the nearest one. And remember that other factors (such as variations in tofu moisture, thickness of sliced vegetables, etc.) can affect cooking times. So, be sure to err on the side of checking your recipes for doneness before the full cook times have elapsed, just in case. You can always put food back in your air fryer to cook longer, but if it's overdone, you've just witnessed your own little tragedy.

What do I do if my air fryer is smoking?	▶ Turn off the machine and check for oil residue. Your air fryer may need to be cleaned more thoroughly.
Why isn't my food getting crispy?	▶ This may be due to an overcrowded basket. Ensure there's room to flip and stir the food regularly for even distribution of hot air. ▶ Also make sure you've used enough oil spray and have cooked everything long enough.
What do I do when chips fly up and stick to the heating element?	▶ This can occasionally happen with lightweight items such as kale chips or tortilla chips. Carefully remove the burned or smoking item and resume cooking.
My food isn't cooking evenly. Help!	▶ Make sure to flip and rotate the foods according to the instructions. Remove finished pieces as you go, leaving the rest to cook further. Check the basket often.
My food isn't browning properly.	▶ Make sure to cook long enough, and use oil or oil spray to coat the outside of your food for proper browning.
My recipe doesn't taste amazing. What gives?	▶ Double-check: Have you followed the ingredients list and directions exactly as written? ▶ Are you measuring properly? If you overfill your flour and under-fill your salt, the result could be bland and doughy. ▶ Are you adjusting cook times, in case your fryer cooks at a different rate? A slightly undercooked dish won't taste quite right.
Your cooking temperatures are so specific. I don't have a setting for 392°F!	▶ Every air fryer is different—I have created these recipes at the settings my air fryer allows. However, many of my testers made these recipes at different temps (they'd round down to the nearest temperature setting—in this case, it was usually 390°F) and were able to keep the same cooking times. Check your food often for doneness.

AIR-FRIED AND PLANT-BASED

The first year I had my air fryer, I pretty much just made French fries and spring rolls in it—and I was perfectly content to do so. Why? Perhaps for the same reason my daughter finds my music tastes so annoying—I tend to find something I like and then play (or eat) it over and over! In fact, I'm still not sick of those French fries (see page 60) or spring rolls (see page 70). It also may have something to do with the fact that those recipes were "safe." I knew how to make them in the air fryer, and wasn't in danger of messing them up. However, it's been pretty fun (and delicious) to discover a whole world of additional foods for which the air fryer is perfect!

For starters, you can use your air fryer as you would an oven—anything you can bake, you can air-fry. This goes for baked potatoes, vegetables, casseroles, and even desserts. Who knew you could make lemon bars (Gooey Lemon Bars, page 122) or chocolate cake ("How Is This Vegan?" Chocolate Cake, page 108) in an air fryer?

Another thing many people are often delighted to discover is the ability of the air fryer to roast foods perfectly. The air fryer delivers delicious roasted broccoli, cauliflower, asparagus, etc.—all with that gorgeous browned, caramelized appearance we all love. I was amazed the first time I used my air fryer to roast vegetables, because it really does give you that slow-roasted result in less time (try a batch of the Sweet Miso-Glazed Brussels Sprouts on page 63 and you'll see what I mean).

And last, but most certainly not least, I adore the air fryer for creating the taste and texture of fried foods. You can make French fries, potato chips, zucchini sticks, and so much more, with your new bestie, the air fryer. This, incidentally, is perfect if you have self-proclaimed veggie haters in your midst. Make them a batch of Alethea's Kale Chips (page 55) or Eggplant Parmigiana (page 78) and they'll be singing a different tune. Likewise, if you've got someone who's resisting vegan food altogether, you can woo them with some air-fried treats. I've never met an omnivore who didn't love the Red Curry Noodles with Sesame Crunch Tofu (page 102) or Apple Puffs with Vanilla Caramel Sauce (page 118).

You can even use the air fryer to heat up foods, melt margarine, or crisp up your veggie burger or vegan chicken nuggets. We even make toast (and garlic bread) in ours sometimes. So, have fun and get ready to surprise yourself with all the diverse deliciousness you're about to create!

The Good and the Bad

The air fryer is ideal for reasonable-size batches of anything you'd typically fry, such as Classic French Fries (page 60), Crunchy Onion Rings (page 52), and Sesame Crunch Tofu (page 134). It's also great for desserts that are small enough to make in one go (Gooey Lemon Bars on page 122 for example), or items that you can easily make two batches with, saving one to be air-fried later (such as Luscious Lazy Lasagna on page 80). I even love the air fryer for reheating and re-crisping foods. There's not too much that little powerhouse can't do!

But although the air fryer may (rightly) become your go-to appliance for almost everything, there are some items that aren't ideal. For example, if you're feeding a large crowd, and your air fryer is small, you may want to bake in the oven to avoid too many small batches. You'll also want to avoid the air fryer if you're cooking something that has a very wet consistency, especially if it doesn't fit into your 6-inch pan.

THE VEGAN KITCHEN

If you want to make healthy cooking as easy—and enjoyable—as possible, I highly recommend taking some time to stock your kitchen with healthy basics, and make meal planning part of your weekly routine. Imagine this scenario: You've tabbed off several recipes in this book that you're dying to try, and you're hungry. You go to your kitchen, and voilà! You have everything you need in your pantry to make it happen. And here's the good news—you absolutely can do this. Yes, you! Having staples on hand make it as easy as possible.

Pantry Staples

As you continue to prepare the recipes in this book, you'll get a feel for many of my go-to items. Here are some basics to get you started:

Chickpea (garbanzo bean) flour: This bean-based flour is hearty and versatile. I use it in breaded items, and you can find it in any health food store, as well as most grocery stores.

Plant-based milk: I recommend the unsweetened, plain version for maximum versatility. I personally like flaxseed, almond, and oat milks.

Whole-wheat pastry flour: This whole-grain flour replaces white flour in any recipe. As I prefer to keep my recipes as whole as possible, I usually call for either this or chickpea flour, depending on the recipe. However, you may use substitutions (or gluten-free, all-purpose flour) as desired.

Arrowroot: This thickens sauces and helps bind breading to your food. It's a more healthful alternative to cornstarch, but they work interchangeably.

Ground flaxseed (aka flaxmeal): This is a wonderfully healthy way to replace eggs in many recipes. By combining 2 tablespoons ground flaxseed and 3 tablespoons water, you've just replaced one egg!

Nutritional yeast: This stuff is vegan manna. Affectionately referred to as "nooch," nutritional yeast is a yellow powder (or flakes) that's high in iron and B-vitamins. It has a nutty, cheesy flavor, and is wonderful on popcorn, in nondairy cheeses, and sprinkled on tofu.

Rolled oats: For this classic kitchen staple, I prefer regular rolled oats to instant, as they're less processed.

Tamari or shoyu: Either of these work well as a healthier replacement for soy sauce. If you're not intolerant to gluten, shoyu is a less expensive option and tastes just about the same as tamari. Please note that I use regular tamari or shoyu in my recipes—if you're using the low-sodium variety, you may need to add additional salt.

Cooking oil spray: This is a must for an air fryer kitchen! I usually keep a few bottles in my pantry and personally use the Trader Joe's refined coconut oil spray. However, any neutral-flavored variety will work just fine.

Cooking oil: As with the cooking oil spray, it's best to keep a neutral-flavored oil on hand. That way, your blueberry cobbler won't taste like olives, and you won't ruin your eggplant parmigiana with the strong taste of coconut. I prefer organic sunflower oil, but you could also opt for refined coconut oil, avocado oil, or safflower oil.

Baking-specific staples: Baking soda, baking powder, and vanilla are all self-explanatory items you'll want to keep on hand to make the recipes in this book.

Spice Rack Staples

Spice it up! I recommend keeping these fabulous flavor agents on hand. Keeping them accessible and visible will help you stay organized. I start with nice glass jars and refill them from the bulk section of my local health food store.

Basil: Dried basil is great for flavoring all sorts of dishes, especially Italian ones.

Black pepper: I recommend a medium-grind version, because it's versatile and gives a nice flavor.

Cinnamon: The classic warming spice, you'll use cinnamon liberally while cooking from this book!

Coriander: Coriander is actually dried, powdered cilantro seed, although you wouldn't know that by tasting it.

Cumin: This works well in several cuisines, including Indian and Mexican. Be sure to purchase ground cumin (vs. seeds) for these recipes.

Dill: Although fresh dill is unparalleled in flavor, the dried version is still tasty and great to have on hand for a variety of tofu and potato dishes.

Garlic granules: Also known as granulated garlic, this is a more pleasant-tasting version of (and sometimes mislabeled as) garlic powder. Look for the version that has a granulated (vs. powdery) appearance.

Nutmeg: This spice pairs well with cinnamon for a variety of sweet dishes.

Onion granules: Please see "garlic granules" and apply everything to the onion version here!

Oregano: A classic Italian seasoning that pairs nicely with basil and garlic.

Crushed red pepper flakes: I love using this to add a spicy kick to Asian dishes and sauces.

Rosemary: Dried rosemary leaf is almost as flavorful as fresh, but lasts much longer. It's something I use quite a bit in this book, so be sure to stock up.

Sea salt: Use a little salt to maximize flavor. Even if you're trying to lower your sodium intake, you may find you'll do well if you eat plenty of potassium-rich fruits and vegetables, and avoid processed foods and restaurant fare.

Turmeric: The ground, powdered root of the turmeric plant is very high in antioxidants and anti-inflammatory properties.

Shopping and Meal Prep

If you plan ahead, you can make sure it's always easy to eat well at home. People often think they don't have time to shop deliberately and plan out meals, but really, it isn't so difficult. No matter how busy you are, isn't it worthwhile to make healthy eating a priority? You'll eat (and feel) so much better if you're prepared to make good food at home and if you knock out some of the work in advance. Plus, you'll save money because you won't be eating out—or wasting food by forgetting about it in the fridge.

Here are some of my favorite tips:

* **Keep your kitchen well-stocked with healthy options.** This takes some effort at first, but will soon make life so much easier.

* **Make a weekly plan.** Here's what I suggest: On Friday, write down what you'd like to make for the coming week and create your shopping list. On Saturday, get your groceries. On Sunday, do your food prep for the week by making sauces, cutting vegetables, etc.

* **Check your mind-set.** Too many people fall into a rut of thinking it's hard to do food prep, and end up eating out all the time instead. That may be easier in the short term, but isn't good health

worth a little effort? Plus, most restaurants don't have food as nourishing (or delicious) as what you could make at home. Keep yourself motivated by remembering the numerous benefits of healthy home cooking.

* **If a recipe can be doubled for future use, go for it!** For example, you can make an extra Luscious Lazy Lasagna (page 80) and pop it in the oven after a long day. Or, make a big batch of the Cheesy Sauce (page 138) so you'll have it on hand whenever the need arises. Look for ways to give your future self a reason to thank you—that's really what it's all about.

On Oil

Oil—what a controversial topic! Some eating programs prohibit all oils, while others (such as the Mediterranean diet) extol the virtues of olive oil. All of this contradictory information can be confusing, so hopefully what I'm about to tell you will shed some light.

For most of my twenties, I was an obese vegan. I was trying (unsuccessfully) to follow a zero-oil eating plan, which I found impossible to stick with (I like delicious food too much, turns out). I'd be "good" for a few days, avoiding all oils and sprinkling my salads with lemon juice—and then feel so deprived I'd go on a fried food and sugar bender. It took me many years to discover that I was caught in this binge-restrict cycle because I was consistently unsatisfied with my food. I finally learned that I could eat oil *in moderation* and maintain a healthy weight, and that balance was the key.

I've worked with countless women over the years who've had similar experiences. Some people can stick with the no-oil approach in a healthy way, but they seem to be the minority. I had a client tell me once that my recipes made her feel so satisfied that it was easy to eat less. Another client told me she'd been out with her son and decided she'd allow herself some avocado and olive oil dressing on her salad. Afterward, she was amazed that when they went out for ice cream (her favorite), she felt so satisfied from the salad that she didn't even want dessert.

Still, I don't recommend using oil excessively. My philosophy is to use *just enough* oil to create a satisfying flavor. I always measure out my fats (if I poured oil into a pan without measuring, I might end up with an extra 300 calories!). Usually one teaspoon is all that's needed to make the flavors pop.

So, in a nutshell? Listen to your body and notice how it responds to the different foods you eat. Eat a mainly low-fat, high-nutrient diet and focus on fresh, organic, whole foods with plenty of fruits and vegetables. Eat some fats, but be conscious about them. When it comes to oils, I recommend organic, high-quality ones. In my home, I keep extra-virgin olive oil, coconut oil, and sunflower oil on hand, as well as a neutral-flavored cooking oil spray.

● ABOUT THE RECIPES ●

You're about to dive into a world of delicious, healthy recipes—everything from Thai curries to Indian appetizers to classic French fries. Please be sure to read each recipe from start to finish before beginning to cook, as it will increase your chances of doing the happy dance upon completion. I also recommend purchasing a deep pan that fits in your air fryer (I use the aforementioned 6-inch ovenproof pan with sides that are 2 inches high). If you can't find one locally, look online—you'll need it to make many of the recipes in this book. I don't call for any other air fryer accessories, although you'll want to have basic kitchen utensils, such as an ovenproof spatula or two.

Also, keep in mind that the serving sizes in this book are relative. There's no shame in the game if you decide to eat an entire recipe yourself, even if it was supposed to serve four (I'm personally quite familiar with this scenario). There are so many factors, including what else is being served at mealtime, individual nutritional needs, and varying hunger levels from day to day. So, as always, listen to your body, be happy, and enjoy!

Recipes will include nutritional information, as well as the following labels:

FRY / BAKE / ROAST This indicates which technique you'll be using in your air fryer.

FAST These recipes take 30 minutes or less, start to finish.

FAMILY-FRIENDLY Recipes that the whole family (even kids and vegan skeptics) will love. Please note that some recipes will need to be multiplied to increase serving sizes as desired.

GLUTEN-FREE These recipes are already gluten-free or include a gluten-free option.

COLOR CODES You may be wondering why the recipes have a blue, green, or purple label next to them. For those who want additional help in constructing a balanced diet, I've devised a color-coded system, taking into account elements like nutrient density, fiber, and fat content:

GREEN recipes are relatively low in fat and natural sugars—and high in nutrients. Most people can eat "Green" foods freely with great results.

BLUE recipes are a little richer, but still healthy enough to include on a daily basis in moderation (for example, most people looking to maintain their current weight can aim to comprise their daily diet of about 30 percent "Blue" recipes and 70 percent "Green" recipes).

PURPLE recipes are fairly high in fats and/or sugars and are ideally suited for minimal consumption—for most people, two to three servings per week (or special occasions) are fine. You will only find a few of these in the pages of this book.

Note that these color codes are only rough guidelines. Everyone is different, and ultimately you'll find your healthiest approach is to listen to your body. However, these codes can be extremely helpful for those wanting to eat a light, healthy diet without having to count calories, points, carbs, etc.

At the end of many recipes, you'll also find tips. These include:

* **Substitution Tip**: Ideas on how to make substitutions to recipes, for different flavors or in case of allergies.

* **Cooking Tip**: Helpful info that may make your life in the kitchen easier in the areas of cooking, prepping, or cleanup.

* **Ingredient Tip**: More info on a particular ingredient—usually one I especially love—that's included in that recipe.

* **Variation Tip**: Do you like mixing things up a bit? These tips will provide ideas on how to do so!

* **Air Fryer Tip**: How best to use your air fryer for that particular recipe.

Breakfast & Breads

Blueberry Breakfast Cobbler
18

Apple Cobbler Oatmeal
19

Gorgeous Granola
20

Strawberry Delight
Breakfast Parfait
21

Delish Donut Holes
22

Banana Churro Oatmeal
24

Banana Chia Bread
26

Whole-Grain Corn Bread
27

Smart & Savory
Breakfast Cakes
28

Potato Flautas
with Green Chili Sauce
30

Roasted Vegetable Tacos
32

Hearty Breakfast Burrito
34

Noochy Tofu
36

Garlic Rosemary Home Fries
37

Cheesy Pleasy
Breakfast Sandwich
38

Mung Bean "Quiche"
with Lime Garlic Sauce
40

Blueberry Breakfast Cobbler

FAST / FAMILY-FRIENDLY / BLUE

SERVES 4

PREP TIME:
5 MINUTES

COOK TIME:
15 MINUTES

BAKE: 347°F

Per Serving:
Calories: 144;
Total fat: 4g;
Saturated fat: 1g;
Cholesterol: 0mg;
Sodium: 29mg;
Carbohydrates: 24g;
Fiber: 3g;
Protein: 3g

My daughter, who loves a good cobbler (but has attitude about granola), had to be forced to take a bite of this while I was in recipe-testing mode (she's actually quite the on-point recipe tester). However, after her reticent first bite, she devoured the rest of my portion—granola and all! It's that good. Enjoy this as a special breakfast or as a light dessert, and have fun mixing in other berries if you're feeling frisky. My daughter recommends adding chopped strawberries when they're in season.

⅓ cup whole-wheat pastry flour

¾ teaspoon baking powder

Dash sea salt

⅓ cup unsweetened nondairy milk

2 tablespoons maple syrup

½ teaspoon vanilla

Cooking oil spray (sunflower, safflower, or refined coconut)

½ cup blueberries

¼ cup granola, plain, or Gorgeous Granola (page 20)

Nondairy yogurt (for topping, optional)

1. In a medium bowl, whisk together the flour, baking powder, and salt. Add the milk, maple syrup, and vanilla and whisk gently, just until thoroughly combined.
2. Spray a 6-inch round, 2-inch deep baking pan with cooking oil and pour the mixture into the pan, using a rubber spatula so you don't leave any goodness behind. Top evenly with the blueberries and granola.
3. Place the pan in the air fryer and bake for 15 minutes, or until nicely browned and a knife inserted in the middle comes out clean (aside from gooey blueberries, that is). Enjoy plain or topped with a little nondairy vanilla yogurt. Delish!

Apple Cobbler Oatmeal

FAST / FAMILY-FRIENDLY / BLUE

SERVES 2

PREP TIME:
5 MINUTES

COOK TIME:
20 MINUTES

BAKE: 392°F

Per Serving:
Calories: 306;
Total fat: 18g;
Saturated fat: 3g;
Cholesterol: 0mg;
Sodium: 130mg;
Carbohydrates: 50g;
Fiber: 15g;
Protein: 14g

Healthy, warm, comforting apple cobbler for breakfast? Seriously? Why yes, this is now a thing! Thanks to the air fryer (and a little work on your part), this delectable, satisfying breakfast comes together in under 20 minutes, with only five of those minutes requiring any effort on your part. If you really want this dish to be over-the-top, serve it with a dollop of vegan whipped cream, and/or some candied nuts sprinkled over the top.

De-Light-Full Caramelized Apples (page 115)

¾ cup rolled oats (see Ingredient Tip)

1½ cups water

Nondairy vanilla-flavored milk of your choice, unsweetened

½ cup granola, or Gorgeous Granola (page 20)

1. Make the De-Light-Full Caramelized Apples recipe.
2. Once the apples have been cooking for about ten minutes, begin making the oatmeal: In a medium pot, bring the oats and water to a boil, and then reduce to low heat. Simmer, stirring often, until all of the water is absorbed.
3. Place the oatmeal into two bowls. Pour a small amount of nondairy milk on top.
4. Once done, add the cooked apples on top of the oatmeal, and top with granola. Eat while warm.

▷ **Ingredient Tip:** If you're gluten intolerant, use gluten-free oats. They're available in most supermarkets, and almost all health food stores. While oats themselves don't contain gluten, they are often cross-contaminated with gluten, and for people who have celiac or strong allergies, this is something to consider. Of course, if you just prefer not to eat much gluten, or don't mind it at all, regular rolled oats are just fine!

Gorgeous Granola

FAMILY-FRIENDLY / BLUE

SERVES 4

PREP TIME:
5 MINUTES

COOK TIME:
40 MINUTES

BAKE: 248°F

Per Serving:
Calories: 165;
Total fat: 5g;
Saturated fat: 1g;
Cholesterol: 0mg;
Sodium: 120mg;
Carbohydrates: 27g;
Fiber: 2g;
Protein: 3g

This granola isn't gorgeous in the traditional sense—I mean, you probably won't want to paint it or invite it to prom. However, it's gorgeous in its simplicity and flavor. This recipe is oh-so-easy to throw together but super versatile and yummy. You can eat it plain and topped with non-dairy milk, add it to parfaits, cobblers, or enjoy alongside baked apples. Or, use it in one of my all-time favorite ways—as a topping for shakes or smoothie bowls.

1 cup rolled oats

3 tablespoons maple syrup

1 tablespoon coconut sugar

1 tablespoon neutral-flavored oil (such as refined coconut, sunflower, or safflower)

¼ teaspoon sea salt

¼ teaspoon cinnamon

¼ teaspoon vanilla

1. In a medium-size bowl, stir together the oats, maple syrup, coconut sugar, oil, salt, cinnamon, and vanilla until thoroughly combined. Place in a 6-inch round, 2-inch deep baking pan and bake for 10 minutes.

2. Remove, stir well, and cook for another 10 minutes. Repeat this step, removing and stirring every 10 minutes, for a total of 40 minutes, or until the granola is lightly browned and mostly dry. It won't be totally crisp yet, but will become crisp once it is transferred to a plate and allowed to cool.

3. Store in an airtight container once it's completely cooled and crisp. The granola should keep for at least a week or two in a cool, dry place.

Strawberry Delight Breakfast Parfait

FAMILY-FRIENDLY / BLUE

SERVES 4

PREP TIME:
10 MINUTES

COOK TIME:
40 MINUTES
(includes granola
cooking time)

BAKE: 248°F

Per Serving:
Calories: 377;
Total fat: 14g;
Saturated fat: 2g;
Cholesterol: 0mg;
Sodium: 335mg;
Carbohydrates: 53g;
Fiber: 5g;
Protein: 10g

These lovely parfaits are light enough for breakfast, but delicious enough for dessert. I recommend keeping the Gorgeous Granola and strawberry cream on hand so you can whip these treats up in less than five minutes. They're the perfect after-school snack for kids, or a luxurious breakfast for adults.

Gorgeous Granola (page 20)

1 (12.3-ounce) package silken tofu, firm or extra-firm

2 pitted dates (optional)

¼ cup maple syrup

1 cup strawberries (fresh or frozen), plus 3 cups fresh strawberries, sliced

2 tablespoons neutral-flavored oil (such as refined coconut, sunflower, or safflower)

2 teaspoons vanilla

⅛ teaspoon sea salt

1. Make the granola and set aside. While you're doing that, you can get the remaining items ready.
2. In a blender, place the tofu, dates (if using), and maple syrup. Blend until smooth. Add 1 cup of strawberries, the oil, vanilla, and salt, and blend until velvety smooth. Set aside (this component will last, refrigerated in an airtight container, for about a week).
3. Layer the parfaits (this is the fun and pretty part)! Grab some clear glasses or parfait cups—the cuter the better. Place granola on the bottom, top with the strawberry cream, and sprinkle with the sliced fresh strawberries. Repeat until you have the desired amount of layers. Enjoy immediately so as to preserve the crunch of the granola.

▶ **Ingredient Tip:** If you're using the optional dates and don't have a high-speed blender (Vitamix or Blendtec), you may need to soak the dates in water for an hour or two so that they're soft enough to blend smooth. If so, be sure to pour off all the water after they've soaked so your cream is creamy, not watery.

Delish Donut Holes

FAMILY-FRIENDLY / GLUTEN-FREE / BLUE

**MAKES 12
DONUT HOLES**

PREP TIME:
15 MINUTES

COOK TIME:
16 MINUTES

FRY: 347°F

Per Serving:
Calories: 114;
Total fat: 3g;
Saturated fat: 0g;
Cholesterol: 0mg;
Sodium: 43mg;
Carbohydrates: 22g;
Fiber: 2g;
Protein: 1g

Holy moly, are these holes to die for! The secret is to follow the directions exactly, as the oil-spraying sequence helps them have that crisp-on-the-outside, tender-on-the-inside vibe you want from a donut hole. As donuts go, these are relatively healthy, since they're made without refined sugar. However, if you have a picky kid like me, toss the end result in a little organic powdered sugar. After doing that, I got the thumbs-up from my own personal vegan donut snob, my daughter, Alethea.

1 tablespoon ground flaxseed

1½ tablespoons water

¼ cup nondairy milk, unsweetened

2 tablespoons neutral-flavored oil (sunflower, safflower, or refined coconut)

1½ teaspoons vanilla

1½ cups whole-wheat pastry flour or all-purpose gluten-free flour

¾ cup coconut sugar, divided

2½ teaspoons cinnamon, divided

½ teaspoon nutmeg

¼ teaspoon sea salt

¾ teaspoon baking powder

Cooking oil spray (refined coconut, sunflower, or safflower)

1. In a medium bowl, stir the flaxseed with the water and set aside for 5 minutes, or until gooey and thick.
2. Add the milk, oil, and vanilla. Stir well and set this wet mixture aside.
3. In a small bowl, combine the flour, ½ cup coconut sugar, ½ teaspoon cinnamon, nutmeg, salt, and baking powder. Stir very well. Add this mixture to the wet mixture and stir together—it will be stiff, so you'll need to knead it lightly, just until all of the ingredients are thoroughly combined.
4. Spray the air fryer basket with oil. Pull off bits of the dough and roll into balls (about 1 inch in size each). Place in the basket, leaving room in between as they'll increase in size a smidge. (You'll need to work in batches, as you probably won't be able to cook all 12 at once.) Spray the tops with oil and fry for 6 minutes.

5. Remove the pan, spray the donut holes with oil again, flip them over, and spray them with oil again. Fry them for 2 more minutes, or until golden-brown.
6. During these last 2 minutes of frying, place the remaining 4 table-spoons coconut sugar and 2 teaspoons cinnamon in a bowl, and stir to combine.
7. When the donut holes are done frying, remove them one at a time and coat them as follows: Spray with oil again and toss with the cinnamon-sugar mixture. Spray one last time, and coat with the cinnamon-sugar one last time. Enjoy fresh and warm if possible, as they're best that way.

▶ **Air Fryer Tip:** If you have leftovers and want them to taste as close to freshly made as possible, here's what I suggest: Store the cooked donut holes in an airtight container, refrigerated, for up 3 days. When ready to eat, spray your donut holes with oil and reheat in the air fryer at 347°F for 3 minutes, or until thoroughly hot. Spray with oil again and refresh with a little more of the cinnamon-sugar mixture.

Banana Churro Oatmeal

FAST / FAMILY-FRIENDLY / GREEN

SERVES 2

PREP TIME:
5 MINUTES

COOK TIME:
10 MINUTES

FRY: 392°F

Per Serving:
Calories: 266;
Total fat: 7g;
Saturated fat: 1g;
Cholesterol: 0mg;
Sodium: 120mg;
Carbohydrates: 47g;
Fiber: 6g;
Protein: 5g

*"Healthy churros for breakfast? Have I died and gone to heaven?"
you may be asking yourself. Yes and no. Yes, you're about to eat a healthy,
yet delicious churro-inspired breakfast—and no, you're not in heaven,
although friends will wonder if you're an angel after making them this dish!
I was inspired to create this because I find regular oatmeal boring—but
I could eat this every morning and be quite happy. In fact, the topping is
so delicious it's tempting to eat it plain: Just double the banana portion
so you'll have extra on hand. I hope you love these crispy-on-the-outside,
gooey-on-the-inside bananas as much as I do.*

For the churros

1 large yellow banana, peeled,
cut in half lengthwise, then
cut in half widthwise

2 tablespoons whole-wheat pastry
flour (see Substitution Tip)

⅛ teaspoon sea salt

2 teaspoons oil (sunflower
or melted coconut)

1 teaspoon water

Cooking oil spray (refined
coconut, sunflower, or
safflower)

1 tablespoon coconut sugar

½ teaspoon cinnamon

For the oatmeal

¾ cup rolled oats

1½ cups water

Nondairy milk of your choice
(optional)

To make the churros

1. Place the 4 banana pieces in a medium-size bowl and add the flour
   and salt. Stir gently. Add the oil and water. Stir gently (ideally with a
   rubber spatula) until evenly mixed. You may need to press some of the
   coating onto the banana pieces. Trust me—it's a small price to pay for
   what's ahead.

2. Spray the air fryer basket with the oil spray. Place the banana pieces
   in the air fryer basket and fry for 5 minutes. Remove, gently turn over,
   and cook for another 5 minutes (or until nicely browned).

3. In a medium bowl, add the coconut sugar and cinnamon and stir to combine. When the banana pieces are nicely browned, spray with the oil and place in the cinnamon-sugar bowl. Toss gently with a spatula to coat the banana pieces with the mixture.

To make the oatmeal

1. While the bananas are cooking, make your oatmeal. In a medium pot, bring the oats and water to a boil, then reduce to low heat. Simmer, stirring often, until all of the water is absorbed, about 5 minutes. Place the oatmeal into two bowls. If desired, pour a small amount of nondairy milk on top (but not too much, or the banana pieces will get soggy when you add them).

2. Top your oatmeal with the coated banana pieces and serve immediately. Can you believe this is healthy?

▶ **Substitution Tip:** Are you gluten-free (or simply prefer opting out of gluten sometimes)? No problem! This recipe (and most of the recipes in this book) can easily be made gluten-free. Simply replace the whole-wheat pastry flour with an all-purpose gluten-free flour (in this recipe, you can also substitute a brown rice or chickpea flour). Still delicious!

Banana Chia Bread

FAMILY-FRIENDLY / BLUE

SERVES 6

PREP TIME:
10 MINUTES

COOK TIME:
25 MINUTES

BAKE: 347°F

Per Serving:
Calories: 202;
Total fat: 6g;
Saturated fat: 1g;
Cholesterol: 0mg;
Sodium: 151mg;
Carbohydrates: 36g;
Fiber: 4g;
Protein: 3g

This delicious, nutrient-dense bread will fill your whole kitchen with the love-liest aroma. The additions of chia and flax make it extra nourishing, as does the fact that it contains zero refined sugars or flours. That's what I love most about cooking healthy plant-based foods—you really can have it all! There's no reason to sacrifice the flavors you love for good health, as this recipe will prove. Enjoy it fresh out of the air fryer for maximum happiness levels.

2 large bananas, very ripe, peeled (1 cup mashed banana; see Ingredient Tip)

2 tablespoons neutral-flavored oil (sunflower or safflower)

2 tablespoons maple syrup

½ teaspoon vanilla

½ tablespoon chia seeds

½ tablespoon ground flaxseed

1 cup whole-wheat pastry flour

¼ cup coconut sugar

½ teaspoon cinnamon

¼ teaspoon salt

¼ teaspoon nutmeg

¼ teaspoon baking powder

¼ teaspoon baking soda

Cooking oil spray (sunflower, safflower, or refined coconut)

1. In a medium bowl, mash the peeled bananas with a fork until very mushy. Add the oil, maple syrup, vanilla, chia, and flaxseeds and stir well.
2. Add the flour, sugar, cinnamon, salt, nutmeg, baking powder, and baking soda, and stir just until thoroughly combined.
3. Preheat a 6-inch round, 2-inch deep baking pan in the air fryer for 2 minutes.
4. Open the basket to spray the baking pan with oil, and pour the batter into it. Smooth out the top with a rubber spatula and bake for 25 minutes, or until a knife inserted in the center comes out clean.
5. Remove and let cool for a minute or two, then cut into wedges and serve.

▶ **Ingredient Tip:** An extra-ripe banana is a beautiful thing in this bread—and also in smoothies and shakes—because it adds a natural fruit-based sweetness and removes the need for additional sugar.

Whole-Grain Corn Bread

FAMILY-FRIENDLY / BLUE

SERVES 6

PREP TIME:
10 MINUTES

COOK TIME:
25 MINUTES

BAKE: 347°F

Per Serving:
Calories: 256;
Total fat: 11g;
Saturated fat: 1g;
Cholesterol: 0mg;
Sodium: 165mg;
Carbohydrates: 39g;
Fiber: 3g;
Protein: 2g

There's something so cozy and wonderful about fresh bread, and here we have an easy-to-make, whole-grain, nutrient-dense version that's "baked" in the air fryer! The flax and water act like an egg, binding the ingredients together, and add an extra boost of omega-3s and fiber.

2 tablespoons ground flaxseed

3 tablespoons water

½ cup cornmeal

½ cup whole-wheat pastry flour

⅓ cup coconut sugar

½ tablespoon baking powder

¼ teaspoon sea salt

¼ teaspoon baking soda

½ tablespoon apple cider vinegar

½ cup plus 1 tablespoon nondairy milk (unsweetened)

¼ cup neutral-flavored oil (such as sunflower, safflower, or melted refined coconut)

Cooking oil spray (sunflower, safflower, or refined coconut)

1. In a small bowl, combine the flaxseed and water. Set aside for 5 minutes, or until thick and gooey.
2. In a medium bowl, add the cornmeal, flour, sugar, baking powder, salt, and baking soda. Combine thoroughly, stirring with a whisk. Set aside.
3. Add the vinegar, milk, and oil to the flaxseed mixture and stir well.
4. Add the wet mixture to the dry mixture and stir gently, just until thoroughly combined.
5. Spray (or coat) a 6-inch round, 2-inch deep baking pan with oil. Pour the batter into it and bake for 25 minutes, or until golden-browned and a knife inserted in the center comes out clean. Cut into wedges, top with a little vegan margarine if desired.

▶ **Variation Tip:** Create a Southwestern version by adding minced onion, whole corn, and a diced jalapeño to the batter (and topping with grated vegan cheese for the last 5 minutes of baking). Or, try a blueberry-lemon version by stirring in fresh or frozen blueberries and some lemon zest.

Smart & Savory Breakfast Cakes

GLUTEN-FREE / GREEN

SERVES 5
(makes
10 cakes)

PREP TIME:
10 MINUTES

COOK TIME:
40 MINUTES

BAKE: 392°F

Per Serving:
Calories: 244;
Total fat: 3g;
Saturated fat: 0g;
Cholesterol: 0mg;
Sodium: 466mg;
Carbohydrates: 42g;
Fiber: 10g;
Protein: 14g

These "cakes" might become your go-to breakfast favorite for several reasons. For one thing, they definitely are smart; you can keep the batter in the fridge and whip these up in no time for busy mornings. They're also a nutritionally powerful way to start your day: Thanks to the superstars here (kale, chickpea flour, nutritional yeast, and turmeric), they're high in protein, fiber, antioxidants, B vitamins, and iron. The list of ingredients may look long, but these are quite easy to whip up, especially if you keep cooked potatoes on hand (in which case, skip right to step two). They're also a great grab-and-go item, because they hold together well and you can eat them plain and on the run. For more relaxed mornings, serve these topped with Cheesy Sauce (page 138), alongside some Garlic Rosemary Home Fries (page 37) and fresh fruit.

4 **small potatoes (russet or Yukon gold)**

2 **cups (lightly packed) kale, stems removed and finely chopped**

1 **cup chickpea flour**

¼ **cup nutritional yeast**

¾ **cup oat milk, plain and unsweetened (or your nondairy milk of choice)**

2 **tablespoons fresh lemon juice**

2 **teaspoons dried rosemary**

2 **teaspoons onion granules**

1 **teaspoon sea salt**

½ **teaspoon freshly ground black pepper**

½ **teaspoon turmeric powder**

Cooking oil spray (sunflower, safflower, or refined coconut)

1. Scrub the potatoes (leave the skins on for maximum nutrition) and place them in the air fryer. Bake for 30 minutes, or until tender.
2. When cool enough to handle, chop the cooked potatoes into small pieces and place in a large bowl. Mash them with a potato masher or fork. Add the kale, chickpea flour, yeast, milk, lemon, rosemary, onion granules, salt, pepper, and turmeric and stir well, until thoroughly combined.
3. Spray the air fryer basket with oil and set aside.

4. Form the breakfast cakes: Remove ¼ cup of batter and roll it into a ball with your hands. Smash it into a ½-inch thick patty (it will be about 3 inches in diameter) and place in the air fryer basket. Repeat with the remaining batter, taking care not to overlap the cakes in the air fryer basket (you may need to do this in batches).

5. Spray the tops with oil and bake for 5 minutes. Remove, spray the tops again, and flip each cake over. Spray the tops with oil and cook for another 5 minutes, or until gorgeously golden-brown and cooked through. Remove and serve plain, or with Cheesy Sauce (page 138). Leftover batter will stay fresh in an airtight container, refrigerated, for about 5 days.

Potato Flautas with Green Chili Sauce

FAST / FAMILY-FRIENDLY / GLUTEN-FREE / GREEN

SERVES 2
(makes
4 flautas)

PREP TIME:
20 MINUTES

COOK TIME:
8 MINUTES

FRY: 392°F

Per Serving:
Calories: 218;
Total fat: 2g;
Saturated fat: 0g;
Cholesterol: 0mg;
Sodium: 324mg;
Carbohydrates: 46g;
Fiber: 7g;
Protein: 6g

If you're like me and prefer a savory breakfast, this recipe will be just the thing to kick off your day! Don't let the longer prep time fool you—most of that time is spent steaming the potatoes. But if you make the filling ahead of time (I actually make a double or triple batch) and store it in the fridge, you get a quicker start to your morning. Then, your prep time literally becomes less than 5 minutes, as it's just a matter of heating the tortillas, filling them, and placing them in the air fryer. For extra flavor, be sure to serve these with a spicy sauce. I love them paired with the Green Chili Sauce, but you can top them with fresh salsa of your choice if you prefer. For another layer of richness, you can also add some guacamole or vegan cheese. Yum-o-rama!

1 medium potato, peeled and chopped into small cubes (1½ cups chopped potato)

2 tablespoons nondairy milk, plain and unsweetened

2 large garlic cloves, minced or pressed

¼ teaspoon sea salt

⅛ teaspoon freshly ground black pepper

2 tablespoons minced scallions

4 sprouted corn tortillas (see Ingredient Tip)

Cooking oil spray (sunflower, safflower, or refined coconut)

Green Chili Sauce (page 142) or fresh salsa

Guacamole or fresh avocado slices (optional)

Cilantro, minced (optional)

1. In a pot on the stovetop fitted with a steamer basket, cook the potato cubes for 15 minutes, or until tender. While they're steaming, you'll have enough time to make the Green Chili Sauce if using.

2. Transfer the cooked potato cubes to a bowl and mash with a fork or potato masher. Add the milk, garlic, salt, and pepper and stir well. Add the scallions and stir them into the mixture. Set the bowl aside.

3. Next, warm the tortillas (so they don't break): Run them under water for a second, and then place them in an oil-sprayed air fryer basket (stacking them is fine). Fry for 1 minute.

4. Transfer the tortillas to a flat surface, laying them out individually. Place an equal amount of the potato filling in the center of each tortilla. Roll the tortilla sides up over the filling and place seam-side down in the air fryer basket (this helps prevent the tortillas from flying open). Spray the tops with oil. Fry for 7 minutes, or until the tortillas are golden-browned and lightly crisp. Serve with sauce or salsa, and any of the additional options as desired. Enjoy immediately.

▶ **Ingredient Tip:** I opt for sprouted corn tortillas due to the nutrient boost, but you can use any variety. You can either serve these flautas smothered in the sauce and toppings (this requires something I refer to as a "fork")—or, if you prefer, forego that newfangled cutlery and hold the flautas in your hands, dipping them in the sauce. The great thing about air-frying these is that they're crisp enough to work well either way!

Roasted Vegetable Tacos

FAST / FAMILY-FRIENDLY / GLUTEN-FREE / GREEN

SERVES 3

PREP TIME:
5 MINUTES

COOK TIME:
12 MINUTES

ROAST: 392°F

Per Serving:
Calories: 363;
Total fat: 12g;
Saturated fat: 2g;
Cholesterol: 11mg;
Sodium: 462mg;
Carbohydrates: 55g;
Fiber: 16g;
Protein: 13g

Tacos for breakfast? Why not! This dish was inspired by a very special breakfast my dear friend Kristin Lajeunesse and I enjoyed while staying at the Clarendon Hotel in Phoenix for a speaking event. We ordered side dishes, as there were no vegan breakfast entrées on the menu. They brought us the sides, and we were floored by how satisfying they were—I can still taste the homemade salsas, fresh warm tortillas, beans, roasted vegetables, and sliced avocado. Later, we found out they were notably good because of the Mexican grandmother in the kitchen, cooking our dishes with lots of love! When we went back the next day, these cool cats had put our idea on their specials board as their "Featured Vegan Breakfast," assuring us they'd add it to the regular menu soon. How great is that?

Cooking oil spray (sunflower, safflower, or refined coconut)

1 small zucchini

1 small-medium yellow onion

¼ teaspoon garlic granules

⅛ teaspoon sea salt

Freshly ground black pepper

1 (15-ounce) can vegan refried beans

6 corn tortillas

Fresh salsa of your choice

1 avocado, cut into slices, or fresh guacamole

1. Spray the air fryer basket with the oil. Cut the zucchini and onion according to the Cooking Tip that follows and place in the air fryer basket. Spray with more oil and sprinkle evenly with the garlic, salt, and pepper to taste. Roast for 6 minutes. Remove, shake or stir well, and cook for another 6 minutes, or until the veggies are nicely browned and tender.

2. In a small pan, warm the refried beans over low heat. Stir often. Once to temperature, remove from the heat and set aside.

3. To prepare the tortillas, sprinkle them individually with a little water, then place in a hot skillet (in a single layer; you may need to do this in batches), turning over as each side becomes hot.

4. To make the breakfast tacos: Place a corn tortilla on your plate and fill it with beans, roasted vegetables, salsa, and avocado slices.

▷ **Cooking Tip:** Because the onion cooks more quickly than the zucchini, you'll want to "cheat" the process by cutting the zucchini into small (¼-inch-thick) slices or cubes, and the onion into thicker (½-inch) slices. Additionally, if you want to vary the vegetables in this dish (please do!), simply keep cooking times in mind. If one vegetable takes longer to cook, cut it into smaller pieces or give it a head start in the air fryer.

Hearty Breakfast Burrito

FAMILY-FRIENDLY / BLUE

SERVES 4

PREP TIME:
25 MINUTES
(including tofu
and home fries)

COOK TIME:
38 MINUTES
(including tofu
and home fries)

FRY: 392°F

Per Serving:
Calories: 422;
Total fat: 15g;
Saturated fat: 3g;
Cholesterol: 0mg;
Sodium: 758mg;
Carbohydrates: 58g;
Fiber: 9g;
Protein: 18g

This burrito has it all—savory fillings, brightly colored vegetables, a crispy "fried" wrap, and yummy sauce options. It may seem like a lot of work, but you can prepare the individual components ahead of time and have them ready to go in the fridge. At that point, your prep time will literally be one minute, so you can make up individual burritos anytime you need a hearty breakfast in a flash. Prep time will also vary for this recipe, depending on which sauce(s) you choose. I recommend the Cheesy Sauce along with the Green Chili Sauce. If you prefer to save time, simply add some grated vegan cheese to the inside of your burrito before cooking it, and serve with prepared salsa. I hope this starts your day off with a full belly and a smile!

Noochy Tofu (page 36)

Garlic Rosemary Home Fries (page 37)

Cheesy Sauce (page 138, optional)

Green Chili Sauce (page 142, optional)

Fresh salsa of your choice (optional)

1 tablespoon oil (olive, sunflower, or safflower)

2 small onions, sliced

1 red bell pepper, cored, seeds removed, and sliced

1 cup broccoli florets

¼ teaspoon sea salt

4 large tortillas, preferably whole grain or sprouted

Cooking oil spray (sunflower, safflower, or refined coconut)

1. Prepare the Noochy Tofu and the Garlic Rosemary Home Fries.
2. While you're doing that, prepare the sauces of choice, if using. Set aside.
3. In a large skillet or wok set to medium-high heat, add the oil and the sliced onion. Sauté, stirring often, for 3 to 5 minutes, or until the onion begins to brown. Add the red pepper, broccoli, and salt and sauté for a few more minutes, until the broccoli is bright green and crisp-tender. Remove from the heat and set aside.

4. Assemble the burritos: Lay the tortillas on the counter, and evenly place some of the tofu, home fries, and vegetable mixture into the center of each. Roll the bottoms up and over the filling, then fold the sides in and continue to wrap up all the way until you have four enclosed burritos.

5. Spray the outsides of each wrap with oil. Place in the air fryer (if they're slightly overlapping that's fine). Fry for 4 minutes. Remove from the heat, turn each one over so they'll brown evenly, spray the outsides one more time with oil, and fry for another 4 minutes, or until the outsides of the tortillas are crispy and browned. Plate and serve with your sauce(s) of choice.

▷ **Air Fryer Tip:** There's no law against using your air fryer for multiple items at once, so work that thing! For example, if you're only making one burrito at a time, you'll have some space next to it in case you've got some batter for the Delish Donut Holes (page 22) on hand and want to make a few on the side. Or, if you've got room in your air fryer basket, you can even make the Noochy Tofu (page 36) and Garlic Rosemary Home Fries (page 37) simultaneously to save time. Every situation is different, so do what makes sense for you. For example, you wouldn't want to cook those donut holes alongside garlicky French fries, or the flavors might clash. But when it makes sense to do so, please know you absolutely can shortcut the process anytime by cooking two foods at once.

Noochy Tofu

FAST / FAMILY-FRIENDLY / GLUTEN-FREE / GREEN

SERVES 4

PREP TIME:
10 MINUTES

COOK TIME:
14 MINUTES

BAKE: 392°F

Per Serving:
Calories: 117;
Total fat: 6g;
Saturated fat: 1g;
Cholesterol: 0mg;
Sodium: 334mg;
Carbohydrates: 7g;
Fiber: 3g;
Protein: 11g

If you're not familiar with the golden goodness known as "nooch," you're in for a treat. Nutritional yeast is perfect for adding a cheesy, nutty flavor to all sorts of savory dishes. It's especially important in any self-respecting breakfast tofu dish. Enjoy this simple tofu alongside some Garlic Rosemary Home Fries (page 37) or in the Hearty Breakfast Burrito (page 34), drizzled with a little hot sauce.

1 (8-ounce) package firm or extra-firm tofu

4 teaspoons tamari or shoyu

1 teaspoon onion granules

½ teaspoon garlic granules

½ teaspoon turmeric powder

¼ teaspoon freshly ground black pepper

2 tablespoons nutritional yeast

1 teaspoon dried rosemary

1 teaspoon dried dill

2 teaspoons arrowroot (or cornstarch)

2 teaspoons neutral-flavored oil (such as sunflower, safflower, or melted refined coconut)

Cooking oil spray (sunflower, safflower, or refined coconut)

1. Cut the tofu into slices and press out the excess water (see Tip).
2. Cut the slices into ½-inch cubes and place in a bowl. Sprinkle with the tamari and toss gently to coat. Set aside for a few minutes.
3. Toss the tofu again, then add the onion, garlic, turmeric, and pepper. Gently toss to thoroughly coat.
4. Add the nutritional yeast, rosemary, dill, and arrowroot. Toss gently to coat.
5. Finally, drizzle with the oil and toss one last time. Spray the air fryer basket with the oil. Place the tofu in the air fryer basket and bake for 7 minutes. Remove, shake gently (so that the tofu cooks evenly), and cook for another 7 minutes, or until the tofu is crisp and browned.

▷ **Ingredient Tip:** An easy way to remove excess moisture from the tofu is to lay the slabs in a single layer on top of paper towels or tea towels. Then, cover with another towel and press down.

Garlic Rosemary Home Fries

FAST / FAMILY-FRIENDLY / GLUTEN-FREE / GREEN

SERVES 4

PREP TIME:
5 MINUTES

COOK TIME:
16 MINUTES

ROAST: 392°F

Per Serving:
Calories: 103;
Total fat: 2g;
Saturated fat: 0g;
Cholesterol: 0mg;
Sodium: 124mg;
Carbohydrates: 20g;
Fiber: 3g;
Protein: 2g

Ah, the classic breakfast side—and so versatile! You can use these tasty home fries as a filling for the Hearty Breakfast Burrito (page 34), on a breakfast Easy Peasy Pizza (page 77), or simply enjoy alongside Noochy Tofu (page 36) and steamed greens. You'll notice the oil content is much lower than what you'd find in traditional home fries—this is my way of creating a happy medium between an oil-free version (which I find a bit unsatisfying and dry) and the greasy spoon version you'd find in most restaurants (and cookbooks). Of course, if you don't mind a little more fat, you may want to double the amount of oil I call for, as they'll crisp up even better if you do!

2 cups cubed potato (small cubes from 2 medium potatoes)

1½ teaspoons oil (olive or sunflower)

3 medium cloves garlic, minced or pressed

¼ teaspoon sea salt

¼ teaspoon onion granules

⅛ teaspoon freshly ground black pepper

Cooking oil spray (sunflower, safflower, or refined coconut)

½ tablespoon dried rosemary or fresh rosemary, minced

1. In a medium bowl, toss the potatoes with the oil, garlic, salt, onion granules, and black pepper. Stir to evenly coat the potatoes with the seasonings. Place the potato mixture in the air fryer basket and roast for 8 minutes. Set the bowl aside.

2. Remove, shake the basket or stir the contents and cook for another 8 minutes, or until the potatoes are tender and nicely browned. Add the potatoes back to the bowl and spray with oil. Add the rosemary, toss, and serve immediately.

▶ **Variation Tip:** You can spice things up by doing different takes on this recipe. For example, throw an Indian-inspired version together by using turmeric, coriander, cumin, and cayenne instead of the rosemary. Or create a smoky Mexican-style version with chipotle, lime, and cumin (once again omitting the rosemary).

Cheesy Pleasy Breakfast Sandwich

FAST / FAMILY-FRIENDLY / BLUE

SERVES 2

PREP TIME:
15 MINUTES
(including
Cheesy Sauce)

COOK TIME:
13 MINUTES

BAKE: 392°F

Per Serving:
Calories: 199;
Total fat: 8g;
Saturated fat: 1g;
Cholesterol: 0mg;
Sodium: 522mg;
Carbohydrates: 21g;
Fiber: 6g;
Protein: 15g

I've been making this humble, unpretentious, oddly satisfying sandwich for decades, and I still love it just as much today as I ever did. It's easy, quick, and darn tasty. The tofu comes together in a flash, and you have all kinds of options for the rest of your sandwich. If you're using a vegan breakfast meat, keep in mind that the different kinds cook at varying rates, so you'll want to get a feel for how long it takes for future reference. For example, tempeh bacon will cook more quickly than a thicker vegan sausage patty. And keep in mind, this is your breakfast sandwich—you can make it as quick and simple as you like or do it up with all the toppings. Have fun experimenting to find your favorite combination!

1 (8-ounce) package firm or extra-firm tofu, thinly sliced into rectangles or squares

2 teaspoons nutritional yeast, divided

¼ teaspoon sea salt, divided

⅛ teaspoon freshly ground black pepper, divided

Cooking oil spray (sunflower, safflower, or refined coconut)

4 slices bread

Cheesy Sauce (page 138)

Vegan tempeh bacon (optional)

Vegan mayo, your choice (optional)

Leaf lettuce, dill pickles, and thinly sliced red onion (optional)

1. Place the tofu slices in a single layer on a plate and sprinkle evenly with 1 teaspoon nutritional yeast, ⅛ teaspoon salt, and ¹⁄₁₆ teaspoon pepper. Turn over and sprinkle the remaining yeast, salt, and pepper on top.

2. Spray the air fryer basket with the oil and place the tofu pieces in a single layer in the basket. Spray the tops with the oil. Bake for 7 minutes.

3. While the tofu is cooking, prepare your optional additions.
4. After the tofu has cooked for 7 minutes, flip each piece over and spray again with oil. Bake for an additional 6 minutes, or until golden and lightly crisp.
5. Toast the bread, and top with the tofu slices, Cheesy Sauce, vegan meat (if using), and any additional toppings. Devour immediately.

▷ **Ingredient Tip:** If you prefer a more "eggy" taste, you can use black salt (aka kala namak) instead of the sea salt. For the bread, feel free to substitute two English muffins, halved, for a more traditional breakfast sandwich. And although the tempeh bacon is optional, I recommend using it because it's one of the few vegan "meats" that's also a healthy, delicious whole food! If you do use it (or another vegan meat), place it in the air fryer with the tofu (gently lay it on top or to the side) and cook until crisp and nicely browned, keeping an eye on it for doneness. Finally, if you're wondering what kind of vegan mayo to use, I prefer the reduced-fat Vegenaise from Follow Your Heart—it's made with healthier oils, is much lower in fat, and still tastes great

Mung Bean "Quiche"
with Lime Garlic Sauce

GLUTEN-FREE / GREEN

SERVES 2

PREP TIME:
5 MINUTES
(plus overnight
soaking)

COOK TIME:
15 MINUTES

BAKE: 392°F

Per Serving:
Calories: 204;
Total fat: 1g;
Saturated fat: 0g;
Cholesterol: 0mg;
Sodium: 580mg;
Carbohydrates: 38g;
Fiber: 9g;
Protein: 14g

This "quiche" isn't something you'll want to serve at fancy Sunday brunches, but it may become your new best friend if you're looking for a protein-rich, high-fiber, savory breakfast that'll help you stay trim and energized. It's based on the concept of fried Korean mung bean pancakes, but it's made lower in fat here (and easier to prepare) by baking it in the air fryer. Be sure to drizzle it with the sauce, as the "quiche" itself is rather mild in flavor. Feel free to add additional vegetables if you like, such as grated carrots and thinly sliced shiitake mushrooms.

For the lime garlic sauce

2 teaspoons tamari or shoyu

1 teaspoon fresh lime juice

1 large garlic clove, minced or pressed

Dash red chili flakes

For the "quiche"

½ cup mung beans

½ cup water

¼ teaspoon sea salt

⅛ teaspoon freshly ground black pepper

½ cup minced onion

1 scallion, trimmed and chopped

Cooking oil spray (sunflower, safflower, or refined coconut)

To make the sauce

In a small bowl, add the tamari, lime juice, garlic, and chili flakes and stir to combine. Set aside. This can either be done while the tofu is cooking or the night before. If you opt for the latter, just store in an airtight container in the refrigerator.

To make the "quiche"

1. Soak the mung beans in plenty of water to cover overnight, or for about 8 hours. Drain the mung beans, rinse, and set aside.
2. Preheat the air fryer with the 6-inch round, 2-inch deep baking pan inside for 2 minutes.

3. Place the soaked, drained beans in a blender with the water, salt, and pepper. Blend until smooth. Stir in the onion and scallion, but do not blend.

4. Spray the preheated pan with a little oil spray and pour the batter into the oiled pan. Bake for 15 minutes, or until golden-browned and a knife inserted in the center comes out clean.

5. Once cooked through, cut the "quiche" into quarters and serve drizzled with the sauce.

▶ **Variation Tip:** I've purposely kept this dish very low in fat, as it can be nice to start your day with something extra light and "clean." However, if you'd prefer a richer flavor, add a little neutral-flavored oil to the batter—or coat the baking pan with a bit more oil. When making the pan-fried version of Korean mung bean pancakes (which inspired this recipe), I've noticed they taste better when more oil is used in the pan (surprise, surprise, right?). So, I'll leave this up to your discretion, as everyone's tolerance and preference for fats is a bit different.

chapter 3

Sides & Snacks

Addictive Zucchini Sticks
44

Simple Roasted Zucchini
45

Tamari Roasted Eggplant
46

Balsamic Glazed Carrots
47

(Air) Fried Green Tomatoes
48

Low-Fat, High-Flavor
Buffalo Cauliflower
50

Crunchy Onion Rings
52

Roasted Shishito Peppers
with Lime
54

Alethea's Kale Chips
55

Timeless Taro Chips
56

Garlic Lime Tortilla Chips
57

Rosemary Sweet
Potato Chips
58

Classic French Fries
60

Cheesy French Fries
with Shallots
61

Berbere-Spiced Fries
62

Sweet Miso-Glazed
Brussels Sprouts
63

Gluten-Free "Samosas"
with Cilantro Chutney
64

Indian Spiced Okra
66

Save-Some-For-Me Pakoras
68

Air-Fried Spring Rolls
70

◀ *Air-Fried Spring Rolls*

Addictive Zucchini Sticks

FAST / FAMILY-FRIENDLY / GLUTEN-FREE / GREEN

SERVES 4

PREP TIME:
5 MINUTES

COOK TIME:
14 MINUTES

FRY: 392°F

Per Serving:
Calories: 29;
Total fat: 1g;
Saturated fat: 0g;
Cholesterol: 0mg;
Sodium: 126mg;
Carbohydrates: 5g;
Fiber: 1g;
Protein: 2g

These crunchy, delicious zucchini sticks are totally satisfying, yet leave you feeling light and fabulous. They're even super easy to whip up! This recipe was born from the fact that I used to be seriously addicted to greasy, fried snacks. Beer-battered, deep-fried onion rings? I would have eaten the whole basket at one point in my life (even though they made me feel icky afterward). I finally realized, after lots of experimenting, that it's possible to enjoy a much healthier version of any fried treats you can imagine, and they're often even tastier! And having an air fryer makes it so easy to crisp up delicious snacks that feel truly satisfying. It's just such a win-win! Serve these plain or with ketchup, marinara sauce, or No-Dairy Ranch Dressing (page 141).

2 small zucchini (about ½ pound)

½ teaspoon garlic granules

¼ teaspoon sea salt

⅛ teaspoon freshly ground black pepper

2 teaspoons arrowroot (or cornstarch)

3 tablespoons chickpea flour

1 tablespoon water

Cooking oil spray (sunflower, safflower, or refined coconut)

1. Trim the ends off the zucchini and then cut into sticks about 2 inches long and ½ inch wide. You should end up with about 2 cups of sticks.
2. In a medium bowl, combine the zucchini sticks with the garlic, salt, pepper, arrowroot, and flour. Stir well. Add the water and stir again, using a rubber spatula if you have one.
3. Spray the air fryer basket with oil and add the zucchini sticks, spreading them out as much as possible. Spray the zucchini with oil. Fry for 7 minutes.
4. Remove the basket, gently stir or shake so the zucchini cooks evenly, and spray again with oil. Cook for another 7 minutes, or until tender, nicely browned, and crisp on the outside. Enjoy the sticks plain or with your preferred dipping sauce.

Simple Roasted Zucchini

FAST / FAMILY-FRIENDLY / GLUTEN-FREE / GREEN

SERVES 4

PREP TIME:
2 MINUTES

COOK TIME:
14 MINUTES

ROAST: 392°F

Per Serving:
Calories: 17;
Total fat: 0g;
Saturated fat: 0g;
Cholesterol: 0mg;
Sodium: 68mg;
Carbohydrates: 3g;
Fiber: 1g;
Protein: 1g

This may be simple, but it's probably the thing I make most often in my air fryer. There's just something about roasted zucchini that's so delicious and satisfying, and preparing it in the air fryer makes it even easier to achieve that effect! Be sure to cut the rounds as evenly as possible so that they'll cook at the same rate. No need to get out your ruler, but the more you can keep the slices uniform in size, the better.

Cooking oil spray (sunflower, safflower, or refined coconut)

2 zucchini, sliced in ¼- to ½-inch-thick rounds (about 2 cups)

¼ teaspoon garlic granules

⅛ teaspoon sea salt

Freshly ground black pepper (optional)

1. Spray the air fryer basket with oil. Place the zucchini rounds in the basket and spread them out as much as you can. Sprinkle the tops evenly with the garlic, salt, and pepper, if using. Spray with the oil and roast for 7 minutes.

2. Remove the basket from the air fryer, toss or flip the zucchini with a spatula to cook evenly, and spray with oil again. Roast an additional 7 minutes, or until the zucchini rounds are nicely browned and tender.

Tamari Roasted Eggplant

FAST / FAMILY-FRIENDLY / GLUTEN-FREE / GREEN

SERVES 4

PREP TIME:
5 MINUTES

COOK TIME:
13 MINUTES

ROAST: 392°F

Per Serving:
Calories: 76;
Total fat: 5g;
Saturated fat: 1g;
Cholesterol: 0mg;
Sodium: 631mg;
Carbohydrates: 7g;
Fiber: 4g;
Protein: 2g

This side dish couldn't be simpler, and it is a very good answer to a question I've heard a lot: "What do I do with eggplant?" I enjoy roasted eggplant plain, but you can also get creative with it. Serve the slices in sandwiches, along with some fresh basil, roasted red peppers, spinach, and vegan mayo. Or layer the roasted eggplant with quinoa, vegan mozzarella, roasted zucchini, and pesto for a fun veggie tower. Be sure to cook the eggplant all the way through so it's succulent and tender—there's nothing worse than undercooked eggplant!

Cooking oil spray (sunflower, safflower, or refined coconut)

1 medium-size eggplant (1 pound), cut into ½-inch-thick slices

2½ tablespoons tamari or shoyu

2 teaspoons garlic granules

2 teaspoons onion granules

4 teaspoons oil (olive, sunflower, or safflower)

1. Spray the air fryer basket with oil and set aside.
2. Place the eggplant slices in a large bowl and sprinkle the tamari, garlic, onion, and oil on top. Stir well, coating the eggplant as evenly as possible.
3. Place the eggplant in a single (or at most, double) layer in the air fryer basket. You may need to do this recipe in batches, depending on the size of your air fryer. Set the bowl aside without discarding the liquid.
4. Roast for 5 minutes. Remove and place the eggplant in the bowl again. Toss the eggplant slices to coat evenly with the remaining liquid mixture, and place back in the air fryer as before. Roast for another 3 minutes. Remove the basket and flip the pieces over to ensure even cooking.
5. Roast for another 5 minutes, or until the eggplant is nicely browned and very tender.

Balsamic Glazed Carrots

FAST / GLUTEN-FREE / GREEN

SERVES 3

PREP TIME:
5 MINUTES

COOK TIME:
18 MINUTES

ROAST: 392°F

Per Serving:
Calories: 48;
Total fat: 2g;
Saturated fat: 0g;
Cholesterol: 0mg;
Sodium: 199mg;
Carbohydrates: 8g;
Fiber: 2g,
Protein: 1g

I used to hate the idea of cooked carrots. I preferred them raw, and even had attitude about anyone who would dare cook a carrot. However, I was put in my place the day I created this dish. There's something so earthy, succulent, and addictive about a perfectly glazed, roasted root vegetable, and carrots are no exception. These are perfect for anything from holiday feasts to simple weeknight meals. You can also take this concept and apply it to other root vegetables—the reason this marinade works so well is the balance of sweet (orange juice and maple syrup) with tart (vinegar and lemon zest). And these carrots aren't just delicious, they're also a great source of beta-carotene, antioxidants, fiber—and happiness.

3 medium-size carrots (about ⅓ pound)

1 tablespoon orange juice

2 teaspoons balsamic vinegar

1 teaspoon cooking oil (sunflower, avocado, or safflower)

1 teaspoon maple syrup

½ teaspoon dried rosemary

¼ teaspoon sea salt

¼ teaspoon lemon zest (see Cooking Tip, page 123)

1. Trim the ends and scrub the carrots; there's no need to peel them. Cut them into spears about 2 inches long and ½-inch thick.
2. Place the carrots in the 6-inch round, 2-inch deep baking pan. Add the orange juice, balsamic vinegar, oil, maple syrup, rosemary, salt, and zest. Stir well.
3. Roast for 4 minutes. Remove the pan and stir the mixture well. Roast for 5 more minutes. Remove the pan, stir well, and cook for another 5 minutes.
4. Remove the pan and stir one last time. Cook for another 4 minutes, or until the carrots are bright orange, nicely glazed (the mixture is glazed over the carrots, and no longer thin and liquid), and the carrots are fairly tender. Serve while hot.

(Air) Fried Green Tomatoes

FAST / GLUTEN-FREE / GREEN

SERVES 3 TO 4

PREP TIME:
8 MINUTES

COOK TIME:
15 MINUTES

FRY: 392°F

Per Serving:
Calories: 162;
Total fat: 2g;
Saturated fat: 0g;
Cholesterol: 0mg;
Sodium: 561mg;
Carbohydrates: 32g;
Fiber: 4g;
Protein: 5g

To me, this dish is the epitome of late-summer deliciousness. There's just nothing like picking green tomatoes, fresh from the garden (or farmers' market), breading them, and air-frying them to perfection. The tartness of the tomato, paired with a crunchy cornmeal crust, is just divine. Plus, these are so easy to prepare, and infinitely lighter than the deep-fried version. If you'll be double-dipping for a thicker crust, feel free to double the coating—you can always save leftover breading for future use by storing in the fridge or freezer in a sealed container.

¾ cup cornmeal

2 tablespoons chickpea or brown rice flour

1 teaspoon seasoned salt

1 teaspoon onion granules

¼ teaspoon freshly ground black pepper

½ cup nondairy milk, plain and unsweetened

Cooking oil spray (coconut, sunflower, or safflower)

2 large green (unripe) tomatoes, cut into ½-inch rounds

1. In a medium bowl, combine the cornmeal, flour, seasoned salt, onion, and pepper, and stir well to thoroughly combine. Set aside. Place the milk in another medium bowl and set aside.
2. Spray the air fryer basket with oil and set aside.
3. Next, begin breading the tomatoes: Dip each tomato slice in the milk, then coat lightly with the cornmeal mixture, making sure to bread both sides.
4. If you prefer a thicker coating, it's now time to be a double-dipper! Place the tomato back into the milk, and then into the breading again. Coat thoroughly on both sides.

5. Place the coated slices in the air fryer basket, and spray with oil. Repeat with more tomato slices, adding just as many as to create a single layer of tomatoes. (If they overlap a smidge, that's fine—just don't crowd the basket too much or they won't properly brown.) Spray the tops generously with oil until no dry patches of breading remain. Fry for 6 minutes and remove the air fryer basket.

6. Spray the tops with oil again and then gently turn each tomato slice over, taking care not to overlap too much. Spray generously with oil again until no dry patches remain. Fry for another 3 minutes. Remove the basket, spray with oil one last time (no need to flip them this time), and fry for another 3 to 6 minutes, or until crisp and golden-browned. Remove to a plate.

7. Finish any remaining tomatoes in batches by repeating steps 5 and 6 until you're out of tomato slices. Enjoy while hot.

Low-Fat, High-Flavor Buffalo Cauliflower

GLUTEN-FREE / GREEN (BLUE WITH DIP)

SERVES 4

PREP TIME:
15 MINUTES

COOK TIME:
20 MINUTES

FRY: 392°F

Per Serving:
Calories: 92;
Total fat: 4g;
Saturated fat: 1g;
Cholesterol: 0mg;
Sodium: 474mg;
Carbohydrates: 11g;
Fiber: 3g;
Protein: 4g

I absolutely live for a good Buffalo cauliflower, and have tried many versions in restaurants. While delicious, it's a dish that can often be overly salty and greasy. Sometimes it's just a bunch of steamed cauliflower topped with buffalo sauce! Brilliant cookbook author and chef Brian Patton of "The Sexy Vegan" graciously allowed me to use his sauce idea here, which uses chickpea liquid (aka aquafaba) and arrowroot for a lower-fat profile with all the flavor still intact. Grab plenty of napkins and get your Buffalo on!

For the cauliflower

2 cups cauliflower florets
(cut into bite-size pieces)

2 tablespoons nondairy milk,
plain and unsweetened,
plus 2 tablespoons

1 tablespoon ground flaxseed

½ cup chickpea flour

1 tablespoon arrowroot
(or cornstarch)

½ teaspoon garlic granules

½ teaspoon onion granules

⅛ teaspoon baking soda

Cooking oil spray (sunflower,
safflower, or refined coconut)

For the Buffalo sauce

½ teaspoon arrowroot
(or cornstarch)

¼ cup chickpea liquid, divided

¼ cup hot sauce
(see Ingredient Tip)

2 large garlic cloves, minced
or pressed

2 teaspoons vegan margarine

For dipping

No-Dairy Ranch Dressing (page
141), or bottled vegan ranch

To make the cauliflower

1. In a small bowl, toss the cauliflower with 2 tablespoons of the milk and the flaxseed. Stir and set aside for 5 to 10 minutes.

2. In a medium bowl, combine the flour, arrowroot, garlic, onion, and baking soda, and stir until well combined.

3. Spray the air fryer basket with oil and set aside. Remove the flaxy cauliflower pieces (but reserve the milk-flax bowl) and add the cauliflower to the flour mixture. With a rubber spatula or large spoon, stir well (but gently) to coat the cauliflower evenly.

4. Be a double-dipper! Add the remaining 2 tablespoons of milk to the small bowl and stir. Place the floured cauliflower back in the liquid and toss well. Then, place the cauliflower back in the flour mixture. Stir well to give the cauliflower a nice, even coating of the batter.

5. Place the cauliflower in the air fryer basket. Spray with oil. Fry for 6 minutes.

6. Remove the air fryer basket, shake or stir (so the cauliflower cooks evenly on all sides), spray with oil again, and fry for another 6 minutes.

To make the Buffalo sauce

1. In a small bowl, combine the arrowroot with a tablespoon of the chickpea liquid and stir until dissolved.

2. In a medium-size pot over medium-high heat, add the hot sauce, arrowroot mixture, remaining chickpea liquid, garlic, and vegan margarine. Cook, stirring or whisking often, for 1 or 2 minutes, until slightly thicker in texture. Set aside.

3. Add the cauliflower to the buffalo sauce and toss gently to coat. Place the coated cauliflower (extra sauce and all) into the 6-inch round, 2-inch deep baking pan. Fry for 3 minutes. Remove the baking pan, stir well, and fry another 3 to 5 minutes, until a little saucy and a little crispy. Place in a bowl, drizzle any remaining sauce on top, and serve hot with No-Dairy Ranch Dressing.

▶ **Ingredient Tip:** If you're wondering what kind of hot sauce to use here, any inexpensive standard cayenne pepper sauce (such as Frank's RedHot) will do! Full-fat vegan margarine will work best (such as Earth Balance non-whipped or Miyoko's vegan butter). For the aquafaba, use the liquid from your can of chickpeas, or reserve some cooking liquid if you're cooking your beans from scratch. (Hey, check you out!)

Crunchy Onion Rings

FAST / FAMILY-FRIENDLY / BLUE

SERVES 3

PREP TIME:
15 MINUTES

COOK TIME:
14 MINUTES

FRY: 392°F

Per Serving:
Calories: 240;
Total fat: 3g;
Saturated fat: 1g;
Cholesterol: 0mg;
Sodium: 524mg;
Carbohydrates: 45g;
Fiber: 5g;
Protein: 8g

These onion rings satisfy the need for a crunchy, decadent snack, but in a far healthier way than the typical deep-fried variety. If you'd like to make onion rings for more people (wow, that's nice of you), simply multiply the recipe and cook in batches. This recipe is the perfect size to occupy the entirety of most air fryer baskets and will turn out much better if you don't overcrowd the onion slices. Enjoy with ketchup, BBQ sauce, or No-Dairy Ranch Dressing (page 141). Also, don't skimp on the cooking oil spray—it's important in order to achieve maximum delicious crunchiness.

½ medium-large white onion, peeled

½ cup nondairy milk, plain and unsweetened

¾ cup flour (whole-wheat pastry, chickpea, or all-purpose gluten-free)

1 tablespoon arrowroot (or cornstarch)

¾ teaspoon sea salt, divided

¾ teaspoon freshly ground black pepper, divided

¾ teaspoon garlic granules, divided

1 cup bread crumbs (whole grain or gluten-free; see Cooking Tip)

Cooking oil spray (coconut, sunflower, or safflower)

1. Cut the onion into thick, ½- to ¾-inch slices. You should have about one cup of onion slices. Carefully separate the onion slices into rings—a gentle touch is important here.
2. Place the milk in a shallow bowl and set aside.
3. Make the first breading. In a medium bowl, combine the flour, arrowroot, ¼ teaspoon salt, ¼ teaspoon pepper, and ¼ teaspoon garlic. Stir well and set aside.
4. Make the second breading. In a separate medium bowl, combine the breadcrumbs with ½ teaspoon salt, ½ teaspoon garlic, and ½ teaspoon onion. Stir well and set aside.
5. Spray the air fryer basket with oil and set aside.

6. Get ready to assemble! Here's how each onion ring will go: Dip one ring into the milk. Then, dip into the flour mixture. Next, dip into the milk again, and back into the flour mixture, coating thoroughly. Dip into the milk one last time, and then dip into the breadcrumb mixture, coating thoroughly. Gently place in the air fryer basket.

7. Repeat with all of the remaining onion rings, gently laying them in the air fryer basket without overlapping too much. Your fingers will get really goopy toward the end of this process. The good news? You'll make it through, and you can smoosh the coating onto the last pieces once things get a bit messy.

8. Once all of the onion rings are in the air fryer basket, spray the tops generously with the oil spray and fry for 4 minutes. Remove the air fryer basket, spray generously with oil again, and fry for 3 minutes.

9. Remove the air fryer basket and spray the onion rings with oil again. Then oh-so-gently remove and turn the pieces over, so that they cook evenly. Spray generously with oil again and fry for 4 minutes. Remove, spray generously with oil one last time, and cook for 3 minutes, or until the onion rings are very crunchy and browned. Remove carefully and serve with ketchup or another sauce of your choice.

▷ **Cooking Tip:** It's easy to make breadcrumbs yourself—and usually much healthier than store-bought varieties. My favorite way is to throw a few slices of sprouted grain bread in a food processor and pulse until finely crumbled. However, if you don't have a food processor, you can also crumble the bread by hand—you'll just need to be patient as it will take a little longer. Either way, you can make the most out of the situation by doing several pieces of bread at a time and freezing your leftover breadcrumbs. That way, you'll have them on hand and ready to go whenever an onion ring emergency strikes.

Roasted Shishito Peppers with Lime

FAST / GLUTEN-FREE / GREEN

SERVES 3

PREP TIME:
2 MINUTES

COOK TIME:
9 MINUTES

ROAST: 392°F

Per Serving:
Calories: 35;
Total fat: 0g;
Saturated fat: 0g;
Cholesterol: 0mg;
Sodium: 336mg;
Carbohydrates: 7g;
Fiber: 4g;
Protein: 3g

I first discovered shishito peppers in an Asian restaurant in San Francisco, and I've been in love ever since. However, I've found that most restaurants either over-season or under-season them. Here I present to you just the right amount of seasoning for the peppers, which gives their natural flavor a boost but doesn't mask it.

½ pound shishito peppers
(see Ingredient Tip)

Cooking oil spray (sunflower, safflower, or refined coconut)

1 tablespoon tamari or shoyu

2 teaspoons fresh lime juice

2 large garlic cloves, pressed

1. Wash the shishito peppers and set aside. Spray the air fryer basket with oil. Add the shishitos and spritz them with the oil. Roast for 3 minutes.
2. While the peppers are cooking, combine the tamari, lime juice, and garlic in a medium bowl. Stir and set aside.
3. Remove and shake the air fryer basket so the peppers cook evenly. Spray the peppers with oil again and roast for another 3 minutes.
4. Remove the basket one last time, shake it, and spray the peppers with oil. Roast for another 3 minutes, or until several of them have scared you with a popping sound and they've got lots of nice browned spots on them (giving them that well-roasted appearance).
5. Place the shishitos in the bowl that contains the tamari mixture. Toss to coat the peppers evenly and serve. You'll eat the peppers with your hands and discard the stems as you go. Enjoy your new obsession!

▶ **Ingredient Tip:** Shishito peppers can be found at farmers' markets, as well as most grocery stores. Traditionally, you'll hear that one in every ten peppers is spicy, and the rest are mild—but, oddly, I've found that certain stores in my area always have spicier peppers. Since their spice and freshness level can vary so much, I recommend shopping around.

Alethea's Kale Chips

FAST / FAMILY-FRIENDLY / GLUTEN-FREE / GREEN

SERVES 3

PREP TIME:
5 TO
10 MINUTES

COOK TIME:
10 MINUTES

FRY: 320°F

Per Serving:
Calories: 113;
Total fat: 5g;
Saturated fat: 1g;
Cholesterol: 0mg;
Sodium: 376mg;
Carbohydrates: 13g;
Fiber: 3g;
Protein: 9g

My daughter, Alethea, and I get along really well, but we have a running argument. I prefer my kale chips in the dehydrator, but Alethea says they're far better in the air fryer because, in her words, "They have a richer flavor and crunchier texture." It's a heated debate, I tell you. So, here we present her version of classic kale chips (and admittedly, they're quite delicious)— just don't make them when she's around, or you won't get many.

4 cups lightly packed kale, de-stemmed and torn into 2-inch pieces

2 tablespoons apple cider vinegar

1 tablespoon nutritional yeast

1 tablespoon tamari or shoyu

1 tablespoon oil (olive, sunflower, or melted coconut)

2 large garlic cloves, minced or pressed

1. In a large bowl, combine the kale pieces with apple cider vinegar, nutritional yeast, tamari, oil, and garlic, and stir well until evenly coated.

2. Place in an air fryer basket and fry for 5 minutes. Remove the air fryer basket and reserve any pieces that are done: They will be dried out and crisp (there probably won't be many at this point). Gently stir, and fry for another 3 minutes.

3. Remove any crisp, dry pieces and fry for another minute or more if needed to dry all of the kale.

▷ **Cooking Tip:** Air-fried kale chips are delicious, but take some baby-sitting. The whole batch will not dry out and crisp up at the same time, so you'll need to keep a close eye on them every few minutes and remove pieces as they're done.

Timeless Taro Chips

FAST / FAMILY-FRIENDLY / GLUTEN-FREE / GREEN

SERVES 2

PREP TIME:
5 MINUTES

COOK TIME:
13 MINUTES

FRY: 320°F

Per Serving:
Calories: 61;
Total fat: 0g;
Saturated fat: 0g;
Cholesterol: 0mg;
Sodium: 29mg;
Carbohydrates: 14g;
Fiber: 2g;
Protein: 1g

You guys. These chips are freakin' life. What is it about a perfectly crisp, air-fried taro chip that just induces pure happiness? Perhaps it's knowing you're having a healthy, light snack that feels decadent and fried. Perhaps it's the unusually delectable flavor of pure taro root. Perhaps it doesn't matter, and let's just get to making these—how about that?

Cooking oil spray (coconut, sunflower, or safflower)

1 cup thinly sliced taro (see Ingredient Tip)

Sea salt

1. Spray the air fryer basket with oil and set aside. Place the sliced taro in the air fryer basket, spreading the pieces out as much as possible, and spray with oil. Fry for about 4 minutes.
2. Remove the air fryer basket, shake (so that the chips cook evenly), and spray again with oil. Fry for another 4 minutes. If any chips are browned or crisp, remove them now.
3. Remove the air fryer basket, shake again, spray again, and sprinkle lightly with salt to taste. Fry for another 3 to 4 minutes. Remove all of the chips that are done, and cook any remaining underdone chips for another minute, or until crisp. Please note that they may crisp up a tiny bit more as they sit at room temperature for a few minutes, but some may need extra time in the air fryer, as they don't always cook at the same rate. You'll get the hang of how to test for doneness after you make a few batches.

▷ **Ingredient Tip:** You can find taro in Asian markets and most grocery stores. Simply peel, trim off any exposed parts, and then cut the inner portion thinly into slices. If you have a mandoline, that's ideal because you'll be able to create uniform, thin slices with ease. However, you can still accomplish this task with a good chef's knife. Just take care to cut the slices as evenly as possible, and thin enough so that you end up with a crisp end result. What I notice about the "perfect slice" is that you can bend it all the way over without it snapping. You may need to experiment a bit to get it perfect, but that's okay! Time well spent, in my opinion.

Garlic Lime Tortilla Chips

FAST / FAMILY-FRIENDLY / GLUTEN-FREE / GREEN

SERVES 3

PREP TIME:
2 MINUTES

COOK TIME:
7 MINUTES

FRY: 347°F

Per Serving:
Calories: 73;
Total fat: 1g;
Saturated fat: 0g;
Cholesterol: 0mg;
Sodium: 93mg;
Carbohydrates: 15g;
Fiber: 2g;
Protein: 2g

What a great way to enjoy tortilla chips without having to indulge in fried foods! I use sprouted corn tortillas for extra flavor and nutrition, but you can use any variety. Please note that your cooking times may vary depending on what type you use, however, so keep a close eye on these, and check on them every 2 minutes or so. Once you've made them a few times, you'll get the hang of how your air fryer and tortillas of choice work for this recipe. Enjoy these chips plain, dipped in salsa or guacamole, or as part of the BBQ Jackfruit Nachos (page 88) or a taco salad. They're also delicious with some Green Chili Sauce (page 142) or Cheesy Sauce (page 138) for dipping.

4 corn tortillas

½ teaspoon garlic granules

⅛ to ¼ teaspoon sea salt

2½ teaspoons fresh
lime juice

Cooking oil spray (coconut,
sunflower, or safflower)

1. Cut the tortillas into quarters. Place in a medium bowl and toss gently with the garlic, salt to taste, and lime juice.

2. Spray the air fryer basket with the oil, add the chips, and fry for 3 minutes. Remove the air fryer basket, toss (so the chips cook evenly), and spray again with oil. Fry for another 2 minutes. Remove one last time, toss, spray with oil, and fry for 2 minutes, or until golden-browned and crisp. These may not all cook at the same rate, so as you go, be sure to remove the ones that are done. Let sit at room temperature for a few minutes to finish crisping up, and then enjoy.

Rosemary Sweet Potato Chips

FAST / FAMILY-FRIENDLY / GLUTEN-FREE / GREEN

SERVES 2

PREP TIME:
5 MINUTES

COOK TIME:
12 MINUTES

FRY: 392°F

Per Serving:
Calories: 93;
Total fat: 1g;
Saturated fat: 0g;
Cholesterol: 0mg;
Sodium: 153mg;
Carbohydrates: 21g;
Fiber: 3g;
Protein: 2g

Potato chips are one of the best reasons to own an air fryer—it's such a delight to make up this classic snack, and know that you're eating something nourishing and light, rather than greasy and deep-fried! Although this recipe only serves two, please consider it a baseline that you can multiply as desired. Unless you have a large air fryer, this is the perfect amount to cook at once so as not to overcrowd the basket. What you're aiming for is an almost-single layer of chips, without too much overlapping, so that the chips can cook evenly. Please also note that your cooking time will vary considerably, depending on the thickness of your sliced potatoes. If possible, slice them thinly with a mandoline, which will make your results uniform and your prep work quicker. It may take a few tries to get the hang of this recipe, but don't give up! It's just so absolutely worth it to make such a healthy version of this classic snack food.

Cooking oil spray (coconut, sunflower, or safflower)

1 small-medium sweet potato, unpeeled, thinly sliced (about 1 cup)

¼ teaspoon dried rosemary

Dash sea salt

1. Spray the air fryer basket with oil. Place the sweet potato slices in the basket, spreading them out as much as possible. Spray the tops with oil. Fry for 4 minutes.
2. Remove the air fryer basket, spray again with oil, and sprinkle the rosemary and sea salt on top of the potato slices. Spray again with oil and fry for another 4 minutes.

3. Remove the air fryer basket, shake, spray with oil, and fry for another 4 minutes, or until the pieces are lightly browned. Chips may cook at slightly different rates, due to varying thicknesses, so remove any that are done before others that need more time. Also, they will usually crisp up once removed to a plate at room temperature for a minute, so if they look lightly browned, they're probably done. (Better to under-cook at this point—you can always pop them back in the air fryer if they don't crisp up at room temperature.) Continue to cook, checking often, until all of the pieces are browned. Once crisp, you can serve—and continue cooking subsequent batches if you like.

▶ **Variation Tip:** You can use this recipe as a basic guideline to make any kind of potato chip. Try regular russet potatoes, purple potatoes, and Yukon gold potatoes. You can also vary the seasonings as you like. Try salt and vinegar chips, garlic and pepper chips, onion and dill chips, or any combination that sounds delicious to you!

Classic French Fries

FAST / FAMILY-FRIENDLY / GLUTEN-FREE / GREEN

SERVES 3

PREP TIME:
5 MINUTES

COOK TIME:
22 MINUTES

FRY: 392°F

Per Serving:
Calories: 127;
Total fat: 3g;
Saturated fat: 1g;
Cholesterol: 0mg;
Sodium: 67mg;
Carbohydrates: 23g;
Fiber: 4g;
Protein: 2g

Did you ever think you'd see the day when air-fried French fries actually tasted better than the greasy deep-fried kind? It's amazing how well an air fryer crisps up potatoes, leaving you with a crispy exterior and a nice, soft interior. Plus, making these in the air fryer actually means that you can add French fries to the list of nutrient-dense snacks you can feel great about—you're essentially just eating a potassium-rich, high-fiber potato with some good-for-you spices and very little oil!

2 medium potatoes, preferably Yukon gold (but any kind will do)

Cooking oil spray (sunflower, safflower, or refined coconut)

2 teaspoons oil (olive, sunflower, or melted coconut)

½ teaspoon garlic granules

¼ teaspoon plus ⅛ teaspoon sea salt

¼ teaspoon freshly ground black pepper

¼ teaspoon paprika

Ketchup, hot sauce, or No-Dairy Ranch Dressing (page 141), for serving

1. Scrub the potatoes and cut them into French fry shapes (about ¼-inch thick), in relatively uniform sizes. Spray the air fryer basket with oil and set aside.

2. In a medium bowl, toss the cut potato pieces with the oil, garlic, salt, pepper, and paprika and stir very well (I use a rubber spatula). Place in an air fryer basket and fry for 8 minutes.

3. Remove the air fryer basket and shake (or gently stir) well. Fry for another 8 minutes. Remove one last time, stir or shake, and fry for another 6 minutes, or until tender and nicely browned. Enjoy plain or with ketchup, hot sauce, vegan ranch, or any other sauce that flips your fancy.

▷ **Variation Tip:** There are so many delicious versions (try the Berbere-Spiced Fries on page 62). Some other possibilities include salt and vinegar fries (omit the paprika and toss with your favorite vinegar) or chipotle fries (add chipotle powder and finish with fresh lime juice). Have fun finding your favorite!

Cheesy French Fries with Shallots

GLUTEN-FREE / GREEN

SERVES 3

PREP TIME:
15 MINUTES

COOK TIME:
19 MINUTES

FRY: 392°F

Per Serving:
Calories: 189;
Total fat: 5g;
Saturated fat: 1g;
Cholesterol: 0mg;
Sodium: 431mg;
Carbohydrates: 29g;
Fiber: 6g;
Protein: 7g

Oh how I love food that looks and tastes totally unhealthy, but in reality is actually quite good for you! This big messy plate of fries will fit the bill anytime you want to indulge, yet you'll still feel great afterward. Overall, this dish is high in fiber and nutrients, low in fat, and cholesterol-free. If you prefer, you can substitute onions for the shallots, but I do enjoy the slightly garlicky hint that shallots bring.

Cooking oil spray (sunflower, safflower, or refined coconut)

1 large potato (russet or Yukon gold), cut into ¼-inch-thick slices

1 teaspoon neutral-flavored oil (sunflower, safflower, or refined coconut)

¼ teaspoon sea salt

⅛ teaspoon freshly ground black pepper

1 large shallot, thinly sliced

½ cup plus 2 tablespoons prepared Cheesy Sauce (page 138)

2 tablespoons minced chives or scallions (optional)

1. Spray the air fryer basket with oil. Set aside.
2. In a medium bowl, toss the potato slices with the oil, salt, and pepper. Place in the air fryer basket and fry for 6 minutes. Remove the air fryer basket, stir or shake (so that the slices cook evenly), and fry for another 4 minutes.
3. Remove. Add the shallots, stir (or shake) again, and fry for another 5 minutes.
4. Make the Cheesy Sauce according to the directions on page 138. Set aside, or keep warm on a very low heat burner.
5. Remove the air fryer basket, stir or shake, and fry for a final 4 minutes, or until the fries and shallots are crisp and browned. Serve topped with Cheesy Sauce—and a sprinkle of chives or scallions if it makes you happy.

▷ **Variation Tip:** You can up the ante by adding vegan bacon (tempeh bacon or coconut bacon would work well), or a few jalapeño slices.

Berbere-Spiced Fries

GLUTEN-FREE / BLUE

SERVES 2

PREP TIME:
5 TO 10
MINUTES

COOK TIME:
20 MINUTES

FRY: 392°F

Per Serving:
Calories: 205;
Total fat: 8g;
Saturated fat: 1g;
Cholesterol: 0mg;
Sodium: 478mg;
Carbohydrates: 32g;
Fiber: 4g;
Protein: 4g

This is the one recipe in this book that calls for an uncommon (hence, less available in mainstream stores) ingredient, but I hope you'll forgive me. Berbere is an Ethiopian spice, and it's absolutely fabulous and worth any effort to find it. It's typically used to flavor all manner of Ethiopian bean and vegetable dishes, but I've done a fun, snacky twist on it here by using it to flavor the very un-Ethiopian French fry. Berbere can be found in Ethiopian restaurants (most will have it available to purchase), online, and in many health food stores or Whole Foods. It has a unique, complex flavor that might end up being your new favorite thing!

1 large (about ¾ pound) potato (preferably Yukon gold, but any kind will do)

Cooking oil spray (sunflower, safflower, or refined coconut)

1 tablespoon neutral-flavored cooking oil (sunflower, safflower, or refined coconut)

1 teaspoon coconut sugar

1 teaspoon garlic granules

½ teaspoon berbere

½ teaspoon sea salt

¼ teaspoon turmeric

¼ teaspoon paprika

1. Scrub the potato and cut it into French fry shapes (about ¼-inch thick), in relatively uniform pieces. Spray the air fryer basket with oil and set aside.

2. In a medium bowl, toss the potato pieces with the oil, sugar, garlic, berbere, salt, turmeric, and paprika and stir very well (I use a rubber spatula). Place in the air fryer basket and fry for 8 minutes.

3. Remove the air fryer basket and shake (or gently stir) well. Fry for another 8 minutes.

4. Remove one last time, stir or shake, and fry for another 3 to 5 minutes, or until tender and nicely browned. Enjoy while still hot or warm.

Sweet Miso-Glazed Brussels Sprouts

FAST / GLUTEN-FREE / GREEN

SERVES 4

PREP TIME:
8 MINUTES

COOK TIME:
11 MINUTES

ROAST: 392°F

Per Serving:
Calories: 67;
Total fat: 2g;
Saturated fat: 0g;
Cholesterol: 0mg;
Sodium: 276mg;
Carbohydrates: 12g;
Fiber: 2g;
Protein: 2g

Brussels sprouts, I will take a stand for you. I know how amazingly delicious you can be when roasted to perfection and paired with a luscious sauce— and I know how unfair it is when people cook you to oblivion and render you mushy and bland. Yes, this recipe is representative of my undying love for the maligned Brussels sprout—and you should love them, too, for their delectable flavor and high levels of antioxidants, vitamins, and fiber.

Cooking oil spray (sunflower, safflower, or refined coconut)

2½ cups trimmed Brussels sprouts (see Ingredient Tip)

1½ tablespoons maple syrup

1½ teaspoons mellow white miso

1 teaspoon toasted sesame oil

1 to 1½ teaspoons tamari or shoyu, divided

2 large garlic cloves, pressed or finely minced

1 teaspoon grated fresh ginger

¼ to ½ teaspoon red chili flakes

1. Spray the air fryer basket with oil. Place the trimmed 2½ cups Brussels sprouts in the air fryer basket and spray with oil. Fry for 6 minutes. Remove the air fryer basket, shake, and spray the Brussels sprouts again with oil. Fry for another 5 minutes, or until they're crisp-tender and nicely browned (they'll ideally be an odd, glorious combination of bright green with plenty of very browned, roasted spots).

2. In a medium bowl, combine the maple syrup and miso. Whisk until smooth. Add the sesame oil, one teaspoon tamari, garlic, ginger, and chili flakes. Stir well. When the Brussels sprouts are done, add them to the bowl and combine well with the sauce. If desired, add the additional half teaspoon tamari if you'd like them to taste saltier. Serve immediately.

▶ **Ingredient Tip:** To prep Brussels sprouts, cut off the base and remove the outer leaves (unless they look great and don't have blemishes on them), then rinse. If they're very large, cut them in half. If they're small, leave them as is—the important thing is to make sure the pieces are similar in size, so that they cook at the same rate.

Gluten-Free "Samosas" with Cilantro Chutney

FAST / GLUTEN-FREE / GREEN

SERVES 5
(makes 10 "samosas")

PREP TIME:
20 MINUTES
(if you have cooked potatoes on hand; time includes Cilantro Chutney)

COOK TIME:
9 MINUTES

FRY: 392°F

Per Serving:
Calories: 159;
Total fat: 3g;
Saturated fat: 0g;
Cholesterol: 0mg;
Sodium: 280mg;
Carbohydrates: 31g;
Fiber: 2g;
Protein: 3g

If you're like me and adore the flavor of traditional samosas, but don't want to consume them that way (with their deep-fried, white flour coating), these may become your new best friend! Granted, the end result is a little bit chewy and a little bit crispy, unlike the full-on crunchy fried coating of a traditional samosa, but I still find these so appealing. They're light and nourishing, but oh-so-flavorful. Plus, you can make a huge batch of the filling to keep on hand, which means you'll be able to whip up some "samosas" in no time whenever a craving hits, and pop them in the air fryer for a fresh batch.

2½ cups diced potato (about 2 medium potatoes), cooked until tender (see Ingredient Tip)

¼ cup peas

2 teaspoons oil (coconut, sunflower, or safflower)

3 large garlic cloves, minced or pressed

1½ tablespoons fresh lime juice

1½ teaspoons cumin powder

1 teaspoon onion granules

1 teaspoon coriander powder

½ teaspoon sea salt

½ teaspoon turmeric

¼ teaspoon cayenne powder

10 rice paper wrappers, square or round

Cooking oil spray (sunflower, safflower, or refined coconut)

Cilantro Chutney (page 143)

1. In a large bowl, mash the potatoes well, using a potato masher or large fork. Add the peas, oil, garlic, lime, cumin, onion, coriander, salt, turmeric, and cayenne. Stir very well, until thoroughly combined.

2. Fill a medium bowl or shallow dish with water. Soak a rice paper wrapper in the water for a few seconds. Lay it on a clean, flat surface (don't place on wood or any absorbent surfaces). Place ¼ cup of the potato filling in the center of the wrapper and roll up any way you please. I usually wrap them like a burrito or spring roll because I like using circular brown rice wraps. However, if you prefer a more traditional samosa shape, you can use square wraps and fold your "samosas" into triangles.

3. Repeat step 2 to make as many "samosas" as you plan to serve immediately.

4. Spray the air fryer basket with oil and place some "samosas" inside, leaving a little room in between them (if they touch each other, they may stick). Spray the tops with oil and fry for 9 minutes, or until very hot and a little crisp around the edges. Let cool for a few minutes (which will seem like forever), and enjoy with the Cilantro Chutney as a dipping sauce.

▷ **Ingredient Tip:** I personally leave the peels on the potatoes, but if you prefer a more traditional, clean look to your filling, feel free to go ahead and peel them. To cook your potatoes, you have several options, such as steaming, baking, and air-frying. If you're steaming them, you'll want to cube them first. If baking or air-frying, cook them whole and cube them when they're done. However you choose to cook them, make sure they're very tender before adding to the filling.

Indian Spiced Okra

FAST / GLUTEN-FREE / BLUE

SERVES 4

PREP TIME:
5 MINUTES

COOK TIME:
20 MINUTES

FRY: 392°F

Per Serving:
Calories: 58;
Total fat: 4g;
Saturated fat: 3g;
Cholesterol: 0mg;
Sodium: 123mg;
Carbohydrates: 6g;
Fiber: 2g;
Protein: 1g

This is my response to anyone who says they don't like okra because it's "slimy." Sure, okra can have an off-putting texture when cooked a certain way—and truth be told, I don't even hate that. I am one of those weirdos who happens to love okra in just about all its forms. However, with this recipe, okra crisps up quite beautifully, and pairs perfectly with the Indian spices. I usually just eat these plain like a snack, but you can also serve them with Cilantro Chutney (page 143) as a dipping sauce if you're feeling fancy. Also, please note that bigger isn't always better when it comes to okra. I've found that large pieces of okra are usually tough, so if you're able to select okra that's smaller (say, around 3 or 4 inches in length), that's ideal.

½ pound okra (3 cups)

1 tablespoon coconut oil, melted

1 teaspoon cumin

1 teaspoon coriander

1 teaspoon garlic granules

¼ teaspoon sea salt

¼ teaspoon turmeric

⅛ teaspoon cayenne

1 teaspoon fresh lime juice

1. Place the okra in a medium bowl and toss with the oil. Add the cumin, coriander, garlic, salt, turmeric, and cayenne. Stir well, preferably with a rubber spatula, until the okra is well coated with the seasonings.

2. Put the okra in the air fryer basket and fry for 7 minutes. Set the seasoning bowl aside. Remove the air fryer basket, stir or toss to evenly cook the okra, and place it back in the air fryer, frying for another 7 minutes. Remove the basket, toss, and check for doneness. At this point, you'll most likely need to fry your okra for another 6 minutes, but it depends on the size of your okra (smaller pieces cook more quickly). Remove when the pieces feel crisp, rather than "squishy." If you have a variety of sizes in your okra, you may need to remove smaller pieces, as they'll finish cooking before larger pieces.

3. Once all of the okra is crisp, place it back into the seasoning bowl. Sprinkle the lime juice on top, give the okra one last stir, and serve immediately.

▶ **Variation Tip:** Have you ever seen crunchy okra, sold in bags near the chips, at Trader Joe's or other stores? I've had them, and they're not bad. However, you can make an even better version, right at home in your air fryer. For a simple version like the ones I've seen in stores, all you'll need is okra, oil, and sea salt—and you'll just cook the same way I've laid out in this recipe. You can also experiment with other flavor combinations, so get creative!

Save-Some-For-Me Pakoras

FAST / FAMILY-FRIENDLY / GLUTEN-FREE / GREEN

SERVES 5
(makes 20 pakoras)

PREP TIME:
10 MINUTES

COOK TIME:
16 MINUTES

FRY: 347°F

Per Serving:
Calories: 79;
Total fat: 1g;
Saturated fat: 0g;
Cholesterol: 0mg;
Sodium: 191mg;
Carbohydrates: 13g;
Fiber: 4g;
Protein: 4g

These pakoras, or fritters, are aptly named, because they have a long-standing history of being eaten up way too quickly. I remember a child getting chastised (mostly jokingly) during a wedding toast once for eating too many of these at the buffet—and this dish has always been the first thing to go at catering events and parties. Long story short, they're addictively delicious and so full of flavor you can serve them alone. However, if you feel compelled to pair them with a sauce, Cilantro Chutney (page 143) is the perfect choice. Keep in mind, you can store uncooked pakora batter in the fridge for several days, and air-fry them whenever you like. Alternatively, if you have leftovers of the cooked pakoras (miracles do happen—although seriously, this scenario is pretty unlikely), store them in the fridge and reheat them in the air fryer until hot. Also, since these are traditionally deep-fried, I highly recommend spraying liberally with oil spray (as directed) so the strong spices taste balanced. Enjoy!

⅔ cup chickpea flour

1 tablespoon arrowroot (or cornstarch)

1½ teaspoons sea salt

2 teaspoons cumin powder

½ teaspoon coriander powder

½ teaspoon turmeric

⅛ teaspoon baking soda

⅛ teaspoon cayenne powder

1½ cups minced onion

½ cup chopped cilantro

½ cup finely chopped cauliflower

¼ cup fresh lemon juice

Cooking oil spray (coconut, sunflower, or safflower)

1. In a medium bowl, combine the chickpea flour, arrowroot, salt, cumin, coriander, turmeric, baking soda, and cayenne. Stir well.
2. Add the onion, cilantro, cauliflower, and lemon juice to the flour mixture. Stir very well. Set aside.
3. Spray the air fryer basket with oil and set aside. Grab a plate and set it aside as well.

4. Now it's time to get your hands goopy for a good cause. Using your hands, stir the mixture together again, massaging the flour and spices into the vegetables. Then begin to form the pakoras: Take small bits (about 1 tablespoon—the idea is to keep them small, so they'll cook all the way through) and smash them together in your palm to form into a 1-inch ball. Place in the air fryer.

5. Repeat with the remaining batter, making pakoras and placing them in the basket, making sure to leave room in between each one so they don't touch. You'll most likely end up placing half of the mixture in the air fryer basket, and half on a plate to cook later.

6. Spray the tops of the pakoras in the air fryer with oil (use a generous amount) and fry for 4 minutes. Remove the air fryer basket, spray generously with oil again and fry for another 4 minutes.

7. Remove the basket and spray the pakoras again with oil. Gently turn each one over. Spray the tops with oil and fry for 4 minutes. Remove the basket, spray generously with oil one last time, and fry for a final 4 minutes, or until very browned and crisp. Serve immediately, plain or with some Cilantro Chutney.

8. Repeat steps 4 to 7 with the remaining batter, or store in the fridge for future use (the batter will last about 5 days in an airtight container, refrigerated).

Air-Fried Spring Rolls

FAST / FAMILY-FRIENDLY / GLUTEN-FREE / GREEN

**MAKES 16
SPRING ROLLS**

PREP TIME:
10 MINUTES

COOK TIME:
9 MINUTES

FRY: 392°F

Per Serving:
Calories: 65;
Total fat: 2g;
Saturated fat: 0g;
Cholesterol: 0mg;
Sodium: 112mg;
Carbohydrates: 9g;
Fiber: 1g;
Protein: 1g

These are an absolute favorite in our house. For me, this satisfies the craving for a fun snack, while still keeping things super nutritious. I love using rice paper here because it's so darn easy—and also gluten-free, healthy, and light (especially when using brown rice paper). They turn out a smidge chewy and a smidge crispy this way. However, if you prefer a more traditional fried spring roll, feel free to use wheat wrappers (many varieties are vegan these days) or even phyllo sheets. If you do opt out of the rice paper for these, simply follow the instructions on your alternative wrappers. However you choose to roll, I hope you love these as much as we do!

4 teaspoons toasted sesame oil

6 medium garlic cloves, minced or pressed

1 tablespoon grated fresh ginger

2 cups shiitake mushrooms, thinly sliced

4 cups chopped green cabbage

1 cup grated carrots

½ teaspoon sea salt

16 rice paper wraps

Cooking oil spray (sunflower, safflower, or refined coconut)

Asian Spicy Sweet Sauce (page 140) or bottled Thai Sweet Chili Sauce (optional)

1. Heat a wok or sauté pan over medium heat and add the toasted sesame oil, garlic, ginger, mushrooms, cabbage, carrots, and salt. Stir and cook for 3 to 4 minutes, stirring often, until the cabbage is lightly wilted. Remove from the heat.

2. If making with rice paper: Gently take out a piece of rice paper, run it under water, and lay it on a flat, non-absorbent surface (such as a granite countertop). Place about ¼ cup of the filling in the middle. Once the wrapper is soft enough to roll, fold the bottom up over the filling, then fold the sides in. Next, roll all the way up. Basically, make a tiny burrito.

3. Do this a few more times, or until you have the number of spring rolls you want to eat right now (and the amount that will fit in the air fryer basket without any of them touching each other).

4. Spray the air fryer basket with oil and place the spring rolls inside, leaving a little room so they don't stick to each other. Spritz the top of each spring roll with oil and fry for 9 minutes, or until crisp-ish and lightly browned. Serve immediately, plain or with a sauce. The leftover filling will keep in the fridge (in an airtight container) for about a week.

▶ **Cooking Tip:** I like making a big ol' batch of the filling and keeping it on hand in the fridge. That way, whenever the absolute need for spring rolls presents itself, I can wrap some up in less than a minute and cook them individually in the air fryer. Happiness, I tell you. Pure happiness.

Main Dishes

Crispy Salt and Pepper Tofu
74

Crispy Indian Wrap
75

Easy Peasy Pizza
77

Eggplant Parmigiana
78

Luscious Lazy Lasagna
80

Pasta with Creamy
Cauliflower Sauce
82

Lemony Lentils with
"Fried" Onions
84

Our Daily Bean
86

Taco Salad with
Creamy Lime Sauce
87

BBQ Jackfruit Nachos
88

10-Minute Chimichanga
90

Mexican Stuffed Potatoes
92

Kids' Taquitos
94

Immune-Boosting
Grilled Cheese Sandwich
95

Tamale Pie with Cilantro Lime
Cornmeal Crust
96

Ginger Tahini Noodles with
Sesame Crunch Tofu
98

Asian Buffet Bowl with
Crisp Tofu
99

Panang Curry Bowl
100

Red Curry Noodles with
Sesame Crunch Tofu
102

Everyday Power Noodles
104

◄ *Mexican Stuffed Potatoes*

Crispy Salt and Pepper Tofu

FAST / FAMILY-FRIENDLY / GLUTEN-FREE / GREEN

SERVES 4

PREP TIME:
5 MINUTES

COOK TIME:
15 MINUTES

FRY: 392°F

Per Serving:
Calories: 148;
Total fat: 5g;
Saturated fat: 0g;
Cholesterol: 0mg;
Sodium: 473mg;
Carbohydrates: 14g;
Fiber: 1g;
Protein: 11g

I've always loved the idea of salt and pepper tofu, but every time I've had it in restaurants, it's felt so decadent due to the excessive oils and refined flours they typically use. I was completely delighted—and still am—about this healthy version, because it's so easy to prepare and is absolutely delicious. This is one of those dishes I make constantly (sometimes daily!), because it's just so satisfying and versatile. You can eat it plain, along-side some brown rice and veggies, or on top of a stir-fry noodle dish. It's even great as a way to convert salads into main dishes. I personally use chickpea flour to make this, but you can experiment with other varieties (in equal measures) if you prefer.

¼ **cup chickpea flour**

¼ **cup arrowroot (or cornstarch)**

1 **teaspoon sea salt**

1 **teaspoon granulated garlic**

½ **teaspoon freshly grated black pepper**

1 **(15-ounce) package tofu, firm or extra-firm**

Cooking oil spray (sunflower, safflower, or refined coconut)

Asian Spicy Sweet Sauce (page 140), optional

1. In a medium bowl, combine the flour, arrowroot, salt, garlic, and pepper. Stir well to combine.
2. Cut the tofu into cubes (no need to press—if it's a bit watery, that's fine!). Place the cubes into the flour mixture. Toss well to coat. Spray the tofu with oil and toss again. (The spray will help the coating better stick to the tofu.)
3. Spray the air fryer basket with the oil. Place the tofu in a single layer in the air fryer basket (you may have to do this in 2 batches, depending on the size of your appliance) and spray the tops with oil. Fry for 8 minutes. Remove the air fryer basket and spray again with oil. Toss gently or turn the pieces over. Spray with oil again and fry for another 7 minutes, or until golden-browned and very crisp.
4. Serve immediately, either plain or with the Asian Spicy Sweet Sauce.

Crispy Indian Wrap

FAST / BLUE

SERVES 4

PREP TIME:
20 MINUTES

COOK TIME:
8 MINUTES

FRY: 392°F

Per Serving:
Calories: 288;
Total fat: 7g;
Saturated fat: 1g;
Cholesterol: 0mg;
Sodium: 821mg;
Carbohydrates: 50g;
Fiber: 5g;
Protein: 9g

This is a nontraditional take on classic Indian flavors, which are always so satisfying. There's just something about the blend of warm spices here, paired with the cooling, bright chutney that will have you smiling and wishing you'd made a double batch. Speaking of which, if you trust me—and love Indian food the way I do—go ahead and make a double batch of the potato filling so you'll have it on hand. That way, if you've also got the Cilantro Chutney (page 143) ready to go, you can easily make these on busy nights with less than five minutes of actual prep time. These wraps are delicious served with Save-Some-For-Me Pakoras (page 68) and Indian Spiced Okra (page 66) for a truly satisfying Indian-inspired feast.

Cilantro Chutney (page 143)

2¾ cups diced potato, cooked until tender

2 teaspoons oil (coconut, sunflower, or safflower)

3 large garlic cloves, minced or pressed

1½ tablespoons fresh lime juice

1½ teaspoons cumin powder

1 teaspoon onion granules

1 teaspoon coriander powder

½ teaspoon sea salt

½ teaspoon turmeric

¼ teaspoon cayenne powder

4 large flour tortillas, preferably whole grain or sprouted

1 cup cooked garbanzo beans (canned are fine), rinsed and drained

½ cup finely chopped cabbage

¼ cup minced red onion or scallion

Cooking oil spray (sunflower, safflower, or refined coconut)

1. Make the Cilantro Chutney and set aside.
2. In a large bowl, mash the potatoes well, using a potato masher or large fork. Add the oil, garlic, lime, cumin, onion, coriander, salt, turmeric, and cayenne. Stir very well, until thoroughly combined. Set aside.
3. Lay the tortillas out flat on the counter. In the middle of each, evenly distribute the potato filling. Add some of the garbanzo beans, cabbage, and red onion to each, on top of the potatoes.

continued

4. Spray the air fryer basket with oil and set aside. Enclose the Indian wraps by folding the bottom of the tortillas up and over the filling, then folding the sides in—and finally rolling the bottom up to form, essentially, an enclosed burrito.

5. Place the wraps in the air fryer basket, seam side down. They can touch each other a little bit, but if they're too crowded, you'll need to cook them in batches. Fry for 5 minutes. Spray with oil again, flip over, and cook an additional 2 or 3 minutes, until nicely browned and crisp. Serve topped with the Cilantro Chutney.

▷ **Ingredient Tip:** I find that Ezekiel brand sprouted whole-grain tortillas usually break when you try to wrap them. So I always seek out Alvarado Street Bakery brand, since they're much less likely to break on me!

Easy Peasy Pizza

FAST / FAMILY-FRIENDLY / BLUE

SERVES 1

PREP TIME:
5 MINUTES

COOK TIME:
9 MINUTES

BAKE: 347°F

Per Serving:
Calories: 210;
Total fat: 6g;
Saturated fat: 1g;
Cholesterol: 0mg;
Sodium: 700mg;
Carbohydrates: 33g;
Fiber: 2g;
Protein: 5g

This pizza is on weekly rotation at our house. It couldn't be easier to make, and satisfies that craving for pizza in such a healthy way (especially if you use a sprouted grain tortilla). This recipe serves one, because it's exactly the amount you can make at one time in your air fryer basket. Of course, this recipe can be multiplied to feed more people, and everyone can customize theirs and cook in subsequent batches. Feel free to add any toppings you fancy—some of my favorites include thinly sliced onions, sliced garlic cloves, artichoke hearts, spinach, kale, banana peppers, and Kalamata olives. For a final kick, sprinkle with some crushed red chili flakes if you're a spicy kid like me.

Cooking oil spray (coconut, sunflower, or safflower)

1 flour tortilla, preferably sprouted or whole grain

¼ cup vegan pizza or marinara sauce

⅓ cup grated vegan mozzarella cheese or Cheesy Sauce (page 138)

Toppings of your choice

1. Spray the air fryer basket with oil. Place the tortilla in the air fryer basket. If the tortilla is a little bigger than the base, no probs! Simply fold the edges up a bit to form a semblance of a "crust."
2. Pour the sauce in the center, and evenly distribute it around the tortilla "crust" (I like to use the back of a spoon for this purpose).
3. Sprinkle evenly with vegan cheese, and add your toppings. Bake for 9 minutes, or until nicely browned. Remove carefully, cut into four pieces, and enjoy.

▶ **Variation Tip:** For a gluten-free version, use a brown rice tortilla. Create a Mexican pizza with Cheesy Sauce and black beans—and then top with fresh tomatoes, cilantro, red onions, and a little Green Chili Sauce (page 142). You can even air-fry the tortilla by itself until crisp and browned, and then top with hummus, spinach, basil, Kalamata olives, and tomatoes for a Greek-inspired pizza. Get creative and have fun!

Eggplant Parmigiana

FAMILY-FRIENDLY / GLUTEN-FREE / BLUE

SERVES 4

PREP TIME:
15 MINUTES

COOK TIME:
40 MINUTES

FRY: 392°F

Per Serving:
Calories: 217;
Total fat: 9g;
Saturated fat: 1g;
Cholesterol: 0mg;
Sodium: 903mg;
Carbohydrates: 38g;
Fiber: 10g;
Protein: 9g

This dish is a celebration of how scrumptious a humble vegetable can be when prepared with love and air-fried. Eggplant takes on a delicious, super-crunchy, gluten-free coating in this dish, and results in something that seems decadent and fried, but is actually quite good for you. To keep with the gluten-free theme, you can serve this over brown rice pasta (I recommend Jovial brand capellini) and extra marinara sauce for a hearty meal. In fact, you'll have time to cook your pasta al dente while the eggplant is in the air fryer. Or, make up a sandwich with fresh basil, spinach, marinara sauce, and several slices of the cooked eggplant. Yum!

1 medium eggplant (about 1 pound), sliced into ½-inch-thick rounds

2 tablespoons tamari or shoyu

3 tablespoons nondairy milk, plain and unsweetened

1 cup chickpea flour (see Substitution Tip)

1 tablespoon dried basil

1 tablespoon dried oregano

2 teaspoons garlic granules

2 teaspoons onion granules

½ teaspoon sea salt

½ teaspoon freshly ground black pepper

Cooking oil spray (sunflower, safflower, or refined coconut)

Vegan marinara sauce (your choice)

Shredded vegan cheese (preferably mozzarella; see Ingredient Tip)

1. Place the eggplant slices in a large bowl, and pour the tamari and milk over the top. Turn the pieces over to coat them as evenly as possible with the liquids. Set aside.
2. Make the coating: In a medium bowl, combine the flour, basil, oregano, garlic, onion, salt, and pepper and stir well. Set aside.
3. Spray the air fryer basket with oil and set aside.
4. Stir the eggplant slices again and transfer them to a plate (stacking is fine). Do not discard the liquid in the bowl.

5. Bread the eggplant by tossing an eggplant round in the flour mixture. Then, dip in the liquid again. Double up on the coating by placing the eggplant again in the flour mixture, making sure that all sides are nicely breaded. Place in the air fryer basket.

6. Repeat with enough eggplant rounds to make a (mostly) single layer in the air fryer basket. (You'll need to cook it in batches, so that you don't have too much overlap and it cooks perfectly.)

7. Spray the tops of the eggplant with enough oil so that you no longer see dry patches in the coating. Fry for 8 minutes. Remove the air fryer basket and spray the tops again. Turn each piece over, again taking care not to overlap the rounds too much. Spray the tops with oil, again making sure that no dry patches remain. Fry for another 8 minutes, or until nicely browned and crisp.

8. Repeat steps 5 to 7 one more time, or until all of the eggplant is crisp and browned.

9. Finally, place half of the eggplant in a 6-inch round, 2-inch deep baking pan and top with marinara sauce and a sprinkle of vegan cheese. Fry for 3 minutes, or until the sauce is hot and cheese is melted (be careful not to overcook, or the eggplant edges will burn). Serve immediately, plain or over pasta. Otherwise, you can store the eggplant in the fridge for several days and then make a fresh batch whenever the mood strikes by repeating this step!

▷ **Substitution Tip:** If you're not into chickpea flour (or are dying to make this and don't have it on hand), feel free to try an equal amount of another type of flour. Some that might work well include brown rice flour, whole-wheat pastry, or regular unbleached white. I personally like the chickpea flour here because of its nutritional profile and hearty consistency, but you may prefer another variety, and that's okay!

▷ **Ingredient Tip:** I haven't found a whole-food substitute for vegan mozzarella that works quite as well in this dish; if you prefer not to use packaged vegan cheese, simply omit.

Luscious Lazy Lasagna

FAST / FAMILY-FRIENDLY / GLUTEN-FREE / BLUE

SERVES 4

PREP TIME:
15 MINUTES

COOK TIME:
15 MINUTES

BAKE: 347°F

Per Serving:
Calories: 317;
Total fat: 8g;
Saturated fat: 1g;
Cholesterol: 0mg;
Sodium: 1203mg;
Carbohydrates: 46g;
Fiber: 4g;
Protein: 20g

This delicious dish is far easier to throw together than your average lasagna, and is especially nutritious if you use bean-based lasagna noodles. (I like Explore Cuisine brand organic green lentil lasagna noodles—however, please note that although the package says "no boil" you'll still want to cook them until a little firmer than al dente, as stated in my recipe instructions). Plus, you have the added benefits of iron-rich spinach, immune-boosting garlic, and protein-rich tofu—without the typical cholesterol and sky-high fat content of traditional lasagna. Plus, there's the deliciousness factor we've got going here—there's something so comforting and satisfying about this lasagna that absolutely, positively warms the soul. This has not been scientifically proven, however, so don't ask for data.

8 ounces lasagna noodles, preferably bean-based, but any kind will do

1 tablespoon extra-virgin olive oil

2 cups crumbled extra-firm tofu, drained and water squeezed out

2 cups loosely packed fresh spinach

2 tablespoons nutritional yeast

2 tablespoons fresh lemon juice

1 teaspoon onion granules

1 teaspoon sea salt

⅛ teaspoon freshly ground black pepper

4 large garlic cloves, minced or pressed

2 cups vegan pasta sauce, your choice

½ cup shredded vegan cheese (preferably mozzarella)

1. Cook the noodles until a little firmer than al dente (they'll get a little softer after you air-fry them in the lasagna). Drain and set aside.

2. While the noodles are cooking, make the filling. In a large pan over medium-high heat, add the olive oil, tofu, and spinach. Stir-fry for a minute, then add the nutritional yeast, lemon juice, onion, salt, pepper, and garlic. Stir well and cook just until the spinach is nicely wilted. Remove from heat.

3. To make half a batch (one 6-inch round, 2-inch deep baking pan) of lasagna: Spread a thin layer of pasta sauce in the baking pan. Layer 2 or 3 lasagna noodles on top of the sauce. Top with a little more sauce and some of the tofu mixture. Place another 2 or 3 noodles on top, and add another layer of sauce and then another layer of tofu. Finish with a layer of noodles, and then a final layer of sauce. Sprinkle about half of the vegan cheese on top (omit if you prefer; see the Ingredient Tip from the Eggplant Parmigiana on page 79).

4. Place the pan in the air fryer and bake for 15 minutes, or until the noodles are browning around the edges and the cheese is melted. Cut and serve.

5. If making the entire recipe now, repeat steps 3 and 4 (see Cooking Tip).

▷ **Cooking Tip:** Please note that you'll need to make this recipe in two batches. If you're serving four people all at once, you'll want to repeat steps 3 and 4 once your first batch is done. However, if you're only serving one or two people when you make this, you'll prepare a second lasagna for another day after cooking your first batch. In that case, layer up your second lasagna as outlined in step 3 and then store it in the fridge (covered) for up to 4 or 5 days, and air-fry it whenever you're ready for another fresh-from-the-"oven" batch.

Pasta with Creamy Cauliflower Sauce

**FAST / FAMILY-FRIENDLY / GLUTEN-FREE
(WITH GLUTEN-FREE PASTA) / GREEN**

SERVES 4

PREP TIME:
10 MINUTES

COOK TIME:
18 MINUTES

ROAST: 392°F

Per Serving:
Calories: 341;
Total fat: 9g;
Saturated fat: 1g;
Cholesterol: 0mg;
Sodium: 312mg;
Carbohydrates: 51g;
Fiber: 6g;
Protein: 14g

This dish is a staple in my household! I always make a double batch of the sauce and keep it on hand for busy days—it's so easy to pull together a delicious meal by cooking some pasta and tossing it with this creamy sauce. You can also add variety and color to this dish by topping it with steamed veggies such as broccoli florets, asparagus, and roasted red peppers. This sauce is meant to be reminiscent of Alfredo sauce (which I was obsessed with as a teenager, during my first job as a hostess at Olive Garden), but this is obviously a much lighter, nutrient-dense version. If you become obsessed with this sauce—as you rightfully should!—you can also use it to top baked potatoes or whole grains.

4 cups cauliflower florets

Cooking oil spray (sunflower, safflower, or refined coconut)

1 medium onion, chopped

8 ounces pasta, your choice (about 4 cups cooked; use gluten-free pasta if desired)

Fresh chives or scallion tops, for garnish

½ cup raw cashew pieces (see Ingredient Tip)

1½ cups water

1 tablespoon nutritional yeast

2 large garlic cloves, peeled

2 tablespoons fresh lemon juice

1½ teaspoons sea salt

¼ teaspoon freshly ground black pepper

1. Place the cauliflower in the air fryer basket, spritz the tops with oil spray, and roast for 8 minutes. Remove the air fryer basket, stir, and add the onion. Spritz with oil again and roast for another 10 minutes, or until the cauliflower is browned and the onions are tender.
2. While the vegetables are roasting in the air fryer, cook the pasta according to the package directions and mince the chives or scallions. Set aside.

3. In a blender jar, place the roasted cauliflower and onions along with the cashews, water, nutritional yeast, garlic, lemon, salt, and pepper. Blend well, until very smooth and creamy. Serve a generous portion of the sauce on top of the warm pasta, and top with the minced chives or scallions. The sauce will store, refrigerated in an airtight container, for about a week.

▶ **Ingredient Tip:** If you don't have a high-speed blender (such as a Vitamix or Blendtec), you'll need to soak the cashews in water for a few hours to soften them. When ready to use, drain and add them to your blender. I've called for cashew pieces here because they tend to be less expensive and I'm always just blending them up anyway! However, if you're using whole cashews, make sure to use just a little more as they'll measure differently. Cashews are a great source of iron and healthy fats—and are actually lower in overall fat content than other nuts.

Lemony Lentils with "Fried" Onions

GLUTEN-FREE / GREEN

SERVES 4

PREP TIME:
10 MINUTES

COOK TIME:
30 MINUTES

FRY: 392°F

Per Serving:
Calories: 220;
Total fat: 1g;
Saturated fat: 0g;
Cholesterol: 0mg;
Sodium: 477mg;
Carbohydrates: 39g;
Fiber: 16g;
Protein: 15g

This is a pretty—yet humble—dish, perfect for weekdays when you want something hearty and tasty, yet clean and nourishing. I've purposely kept this dish very light, for those times when you want something without added fats or sweeteners. However, if you prefer a richer flavor, you can stir in a little olive oil or vegan margarine. As with most of my recipes, I've kept many of the nutrient-dense items (kale, lemon, and garlic) as last-minute stir-in additions in order to preserve their nutrients and freshness. Enjoy this dish plain or on top of brown rice or quinoa—or with a slice of crusty bread on the side.

1 cup red lentils

4 cups water

Cooking oil spray (coconut, sunflower, or safflower)

1 medium-size onion, peeled and cut into ¼-inch-thick rings

Sea salt

½ cup kale, stems removed, thinly sliced

3 large garlic cloves, pressed or minced

2 tablespoons fresh lemon juice

2 teaspoons nutritional yeast

1 teaspoon sea salt

1 teaspoon lemon zest (see Ingredient Tip)

¾ teaspoon freshly ground black pepper

1. In a medium-large pot, bring the lentils and water to a boil over medium-high heat. Reduce the heat to low and simmer, uncovered, for about 30 minutes (or until the lentils have dissolved completely), making sure to stir every 5 minutes or so as they cook (so that the lentils don't stick to the bottom of the pot).

2. While the lentils are cooking, get the rest of your dish together. Spray the air fryer basket with oil and place the onion rings inside, separating them as much as possible. Spray them with the oil and sprinkle with a little salt. Fry for 5 minutes. Remove the air fryer basket, shake or stir, spray again with oil, and fry for another 5 minutes. (Note: You're aiming for all of the onion slices to be crisp and well browned, so if some of the pieces begin to do that, transfer them from the air fryer basket to a plate.)

3. Remove the air fryer basket, spray the onions again with oil, and fry for a final 5 minutes or until all the pieces are crisp and browned.
4. To finish the lentils: Add the kale to the hot lentils, and stir very well, as the heat from the lentils will steam the thinly sliced greens. Stir in the garlic, lemon juice, nutritional yeast, salt, zest, and pepper. Stir very well and then distribute evenly in bowls. Top with the crisp onion rings and serve.

▶ **Ingredient Tip:** There's just no substitution for fresh lemon juice, and this recipe is no exception. Bottled lemon (or lime) juice tastes "off" to me, and should only be used when there's no other option. Otherwise, please use fresh juice whenever called for in this book, as it imparts such a bright, fresh flavor—as well as wonderful alkaline properties and vitamins. To juice a lemon, you have several options. In my kitchen, I mainly use a handheld juicer unless I'm juicing up several at once, in which case I use an electric juicer. To save time, I sometimes juice several lemons or limes at once, and store the juice in an airtight glass container in the refrigerator for a few days. For zesting, I recommend a good Microplane-style zester, which you can find in any kitchen store or superstore. See the Cooking Tip on page 123 for best zesting practices.

Our Daily Bean

FAST / FAMILY-FRIENDLY / GLUTEN-FREE / GREEN

SERVES 2

PREP TIME:
5 MINUTES

COOK TIME:
8 MINUTES

BAKE: 392°F

Per Serving:
Calories: 284;
Total fat: 4g;
Saturated fat: 1g;
Cholesterol: 0mg;
Sodium: 807mg;
Carbohydrates: 47g;
Fiber: 16g;
Protein: 20g

This simple baked dish of seasoned pinto beans and tomato is so healthy, light, and easy to make that we go through phases of eating it daily. There's something oddly comforting about it too—these rich, mellow flavors just hit the spot somehow. If you'd like a more substantial main dish, feel free to serve this over brown rice or quinoa—or alongside bread, soft tortillas, or Whole-Grain Corn Bread (page 27). As with any meal, I also recommend including some fresh or steamed vegetables on the side for additional nutrition. These beans pair especially well with stir-fried kale seasoned with lemon and garlic.

1 (15-ounce) can pinto beans, drained

¼ cup tomato sauce

2 tablespoons nutritional yeast

2 large garlic cloves, pressed or minced

½ teaspoon dried oregano

½ teaspoon cumin

¼ teaspoon sea salt

⅛ teaspoon freshly ground black pepper

Cooking oil spray (sunflower, safflower, or refined coconut)

1. In a medium bowl, stir together the beans, tomato sauce, nutritional yeast, garlic, oregano, cumin, salt, and pepper until well combined.

2. Spray the 6-inch round, 2-inch deep baking pan with oil and pour the bean mixture into it. Bake for 4 minutes. Remove, stir well, and bake for another 4 minutes, or until the mixture has thickened and is heated through. It will most likely form a little crust on top and be lightly browned in spots. Serve hot. This will keep, refrigerated in an airtight container, for up to a week.

Taco Salad with Creamy Lime Sauce

FAST / FAMILY-FRIENDLY / GLUTEN-FREE / GREEN

SERVES 3

PREP TIME:
20 MINUTES

COOK TIME:
7 MINUTES

FRY: 347°F

Per Serving:
Calories: 422;
Total fat: 7g;
Saturated fat: 1g;
Cholesterol: 0mg;
Sodium: 1186mg;
Carbohydrates: 71g;
Fiber: 15g;
Protein: 22g

This meal is ideal for busy weekday evenings. The Creamy Lime Sauce will keep, refrigerated, for at least a week, so make a double batch if you love it. You can also keep your vegetables prepped and ready to go in the fridge. That way, all you'll need to do is reheat the beans, air-fry the chips, and assemble your salads. On a personal note, I especially love any entrée that helps me knock out half of my daily vegetable intake goal in one go—each serving contains about three cups of fresh vegetables!

For the sauce

- 1 (12.3-ounce) package of silken-firm tofu
- ¼ cup plus 1 tablespoon fresh lime juice
- Zest of 1 large lime (1 teaspoon)
- 1½ tablespoons coconut sugar
- 3 large garlic cloves, peeled
- 1 teaspoon sea salt
- ½ teaspoon ground chipotle powder

For the salad

- 6 cups romaine lettuce, chopped (1 large head)
- 1 (15-ounce) can vegan refried beans (or whole pinto or black beans if you prefer)
- 1 cup chopped red cabbage
- 2 medium tomatoes, chopped
- ½ cup chopped cilantro
- ¼ cup minced scallions
- Double batch of Garlic Lime Tortilla Chips (page 57)

To make the sauce

Drain the tofu (pour off any liquid) and place in a blender. Add the lime juice and zest, coconut sugar, garlic, salt, and chipotle powder. Blend until very smooth. Set aside.

To make the salad

1. Distribute the lettuce equally into three big bowls.
2. In a small pan over medium heat, warm the beans, stirring often, until hot (this should take less than a minute). Place on top of the lettuce. Top the beans with the cabbage, tomatoes, cilantro, and scallions. Drizzle generously with the Creamy Lime Sauce and serve with the double batch of air-fried chips. Enjoy immediately.

BBQ Jackfruit Nachos

FAMILY-FRIENDLY / GLUTEN-FREE / BLUE

SERVES 3

PREP TIME:
30 MINUTES

COOK TIME:
20 MINUTES

FRY: 347°F

Per Serving:
Calories: 661;
Total fat: 15g;
Saturated fat: 1g;
Cholesterol: 0mg;
Sodium: 1842mg;
Carbohydrates: 124g;
Fiber: 19g;
Protein: 22g

Nachos for dinner? And—hold the phone—they're healthy too? Just another day in the life of your air fryer (and some cool vegan ingredients). If you've never cooked with jackfruit, you can find it at any health food store or Trader Joe's; it's a low-calorie, high-fiber food that has the texture of pulled pork and is very easy to cook with. However, if you prefer, you can skip it and substitute black, pinto, or vegan refried beans instead. You can also customize this recipe—for most kids, leave off the jalapeño and onion; for people who love heat, add more jalapeño or another variety of hot pepper. If you want to shortcut the process, make the Cheesy Sauce ahead of time, as well as the BBQ Jackfruit (which will keep in an airtight container, refrigerated, for up to a week). That way, you can make nachos in a flash anytime the craving hits!

1 (20-ounce) can jackfruit, drained

⅓ cup prepared vegan BBQ sauce (I use Organicville agave-sweetened)

¼ cup water

2 tablespoons tamari or shoyu

1 tablespoon fresh lemon juice

4 large garlic cloves, pressed or minced

1 teaspoon onion granules

⅛ teaspoon cayenne powder

⅛ teaspoon liquid smoke

Double batch Garlic Lime Tortilla Chips (page 57)

2½ cups prepared Cheesy Sauce (page 138)

3 medium-size tomatoes, chopped

¾ cup guacamole of your choice

¾ cup chopped cilantro

½ cup minced red onion

1 jalapeño, seeds removed and thinly sliced (optional)

1. In a large skillet over high heat, place the jackfruit, BBQ sauce, water, tamari, lemon juice, garlic, onion granules, cayenne, and liquid smoke. Stir well and break up the jackfruit a bit with a spatula.

2. Once the mixture boils, reduce the heat to low. Continue to cook, stirring often (and breaking up the jackfruit as you stir), for about 20 minutes, or until all of the liquid has been absorbed. Remove from the heat and set aside.
3. Assemble the nachos: Distribute the chips onto three plates, and then top evenly with the jackfruit mixture, warmed Cheesy Sauce, tomatoes, guacamole, cilantro, onion, and jalapeño (if using). Enjoy immediately, because soggy chips are tragic.

10-Minute Chimichanga

FAST / FAMILY-FRIENDLY / GREEN

SERVES 1

PREP TIME:
2 MINUTES

COOK TIME:
8 MINUTES

FRY: 392°F

Per Serving:
Calories: 317;
Total fat: 6g;
Saturated fat: 2g;
Cholesterol: 0mg;
Sodium: 955mg;
Carbohydrates: 55g;
Fiber: 11g;
Protein: 13g

This lifesaver of an entrée comes together in less than 10 minutes! It's ridiculously easy to make, healthy and light, and absolutely satisfying. Plus, it reminds me of my favorite deep-fried treat growing up. My grandparents would take me to a Mexican place where the waitstaff never needed to ask what I was going to order—they'd just look at me and smile, because they knew I never strayed from my favorite dish! Years later, I'm delighted to discover that the deep-fried feel of a chimichanga can be replicated in an air fryer, so I hope this one makes you happy, too! Please note that this recipe serves one because that's how I've found it's easiest to personalize. For more servings, simply multiply these amounts and place your chimichangas in the air fryer basket in a single layer, touching each other as little as possible, for maximum crispness.

1 whole-grain tortilla

½ cup vegan refried beans

¼ cup grated vegan cheese (optional)

Cooking oil spray (sunflower, safflower, or refined coconut)

½ cup fresh salsa (or Green Chili Sauce, page 142)

2 cups chopped romaine lettuce (about ½ head)

Guacamole (optional)

Chopped cilantro (optional)

Cheesy Sauce (page 138) (optional)

1. Lay the tortilla on a flat surface and place the beans in the center. Top with the cheese, if using. Wrap the bottom up over the filling, and then fold in the sides. Then roll it all up so as to enclose the beans inside the tortilla (you're making an enclosed burrito here).

2. Spray the air fryer basket with oil, place the tortilla wrap inside the basket, seam-side down, and spray the top of the chimichanga with oil. Fry for 5 minutes. Spray the top (and sides) again with oil, flip over, and spray the other side with oil. Fry for an additional 2 or 3 minutes, until nicely browned and crisp.
3. Transfer to a plate. Top with the salsa, lettuce, guacamole, cilantro, and/or Cheesy Sauce, if using. Serve immediately.

▶ **Variation Tip:** There are lots of ways to customize your chimichanga, but I'll share my go-to: I like to cover the finished chimichanga with 3 cups of romaine lettuce (to get in some extra-extra veggie love), lots of fresh salsa (I use about a cup of fresh tomato or tomatillo salsa), and a small scoop of guacamole. It's simple, delicious, and so filling!

Mexican Stuffed Potatoes

FAMILY-FRIENDLY / GLUTEN-FREE / GREEN

SERVES 4

PREP TIME:
15 MINUTES

COOK TIME:
40 MINUTES

BAKE: 392°F

Per Serving
(¼ cup prepared):
Calories: 420;
Total fat: 5g;
Saturated fat: 0g;
Cholesterol: 0mg;
Sodium: 503mg;
Carbohydrates: 80g;
Fiber: 17g;
Protein: 15g

These stuffed potatoes are the kind of food party I like to be invited to—lots of fun flavors, vibrant colors, and nutrient-dense goodness that leaves you feeling light, yet satisfied. You can also one-up this recipe and make it into a stuffed potato bar. Place all of your toppings out on the counter and let your people go wild making their own creations. Wild, I tell you! If that's your plan, feel free to add even more options, such as vegan bacon, salsa, minced red onion, crushed tortilla chips, and nondairy sour cream. You can also use this concept to create other "baked potato bars" such as a Greek version with baba ghanoush, hummus, falafel crumbles, tomato salad, and Kalamata olives. A baked—or in this case, air-fried—potato presents a wonderful, whole food foundation to create easy, nourishing dinners that your whole family will love!

4 large potatoes, any variety (I like Yukon gold or russets for this dish; see Cooking Tip)

Cooking oil spray (sunflower, safflower, or refined coconut)

1½ cups Cheesy Sauce (page 138)

1 cup black or pinto beans (canned beans are fine; be sure to drain and rinse)

2 medium tomatoes, chopped

1 scallion, finely chopped

⅓ cup finely chopped cilantro

1 jalapeño, finely sliced or minced (optional)

1 avocado, diced (optional)

1. Scrub the potatoes, prick with a fork, and spray the outsides with oil. Place in the air fryer (leaving room in between so the air can circulate) and bake for 30 minutes.

2. While the potatoes are cooking, prepare the Cheesy Sauce and additional items. Set aside.

3. Check the potatoes at the 30-minute mark by poking a fork into them. If they're very tender, they're done. If not, continue to cook until a fork inserted proves them to be well-done. (As potato sizes vary, so will your cook time—the average cook time is usually about 40 minutes.)

4. When the potatoes are getting very close to being tender, warm the Cheesy Sauce and the beans in separate pans.

5. To assemble: Plate the potatoes and cut them across the top. Then, pry them open with a fork—just enough to get all the goodies in there. Top each potato with the Cheesy Sauce, beans, tomatoes, scallions, cilantro, and jalapeño and avocado, if using. Enjoy immediately.

▶ **Cooking Tip:** Whenever I bake potatoes in the air fryer, I make extra. As long as you don't overcrowd them, you can make as many as you like. It's great to have cooked potatoes on hand in the fridge, because they make a convenient snack for busy times (you can even eat them plain in a pinch) and you can also slice them up and air-fry (or pan-fry) them with a little oil, garlic, and salt. In fact, my grandma absolutely relied on these—she'd regularly make pan-fried potatoes in her electric skillet because she was a smart lady who kept cooked potatoes in her fridge almost all the time.

Kids' Taquitos

FAST / FAMILY-FRIENDLY / GLUTEN-FREE / BLUE

SERVES 4

PREP TIME:
5 MINUTES

COOK TIME:
7 MINUTES

FRY: 392°F

Per Serving:
Calories: 286;
Total fat: 9g;
Saturated fat: 4g;
Cholesterol: 0mg;
Sodium: 609mg;
Carbohydrates: 44g;
Fiber: 9g;
Protein: 9g

I feel like a bit of a criminal giving you a recipe this simple, but it's one of those things I depend on when I have picky kids (or adults!) to feed. As any parent or caretaker of kids knows, sometimes you just need a simple recipe you can whip up quickly that will satisfy the hunger of little ones who lack adventurous palates. My daughter likes these with the bare minimum—just the beans and cheese inside, and served with vegan sour cream. However, if your kids are up for it, you can add additional fillings and toppings. No matter how you serve these, you can feel great knowing your kids are getting lots of great nutrition, including whole grains, fiber, and plenty of protein. For added health insurance, serve these with some raw vegetables on the side to dip in the No-Dairy Ranch Dressing (page 141).

8 corn tortillas

Cooking oil spray (coconut, sunflower, or safflower)

1 (15-ounce) can vegan refried beans

1 cup shredded vegan cheese

Guacamole (optional)

Cheesy Sauce (page 138) (optional)

Vegan sour cream (optional)

Fresh salsa (optional)

1. Warm the tortillas (so they don't break): Run them under water for a second, and then place in an oil-sprayed air fryer basket (stacking them is fine). Fry for 1 minute.

2. Remove to a flat surface, laying them out individually. Place an equal amount of the beans in a line down the center of each tortilla. Top with the vegan cheese.

3. Roll the tortilla sides up over the filling and place seam-side down in the air fryer basket (this will help them seal so the tortillas don't fly open). Add just enough to fill the basket without them touching too much (you may need to do another batch, depending on the size of your air fryer basket).

4. Spray the tops with oil. Fry for 7 minutes, or until the tortillas are golden-brown and lightly crisp. Serve immediately with your preferred toppings.

Immune-Boosting
Grilled Cheese Sandwich

FAST / FAMILY-FRIENDLY / BLUE

SERVES 1

PREP TIME:
3 MINUTES

COOK TIME:
12 MINUTES

FRY: 392°F

Per Serving:
Calories: 288;
Total fat: 13g;
Saturated fat: 5g;
Cholesterol: 0mg;
Sodium: 1013mg;
Carbohydrates: 34g;
Fiber: 4g;
Protein: 8g

I know you've got some questions about this one. Air-frying a grilled cheese? Yep, and it's surprisingly awesome and crispy. And how could it possibly be immune-boosting? Well, when you use sprouted whole-grain bread and add powerhouse ingredients like miso, garlic, and fermented vegetables, this comfort food classic actually becomes quite healthful! Add the extras after cooking the sandwich, to help maximize the nutrients of those raw superfoods.

2 slices sprouted whole-grain bread (or substitute a gluten-free bread)

1 teaspoon vegan margarine or neutral-flavored oil (sunflower, safflower, or refined coconut)

2 slices vegan cheese (Violife cheddar or Chao creamy original) or Cheesy Sauce (page 138)

1 teaspoon mellow white miso

1 medium-large garlic clove, pressed or finely minced

2 tablespoons fermented vegetables, kimchi, or sauerkraut

Romaine or green leaf lettuce

1. Spread the outsides of the bread with the vegan margarine. Place the sliced cheese inside and close the sandwich back up again (buttered sides facing out). Place the sandwich in the air fryer basket and fry for 6 minutes. Flip over and fry for another 6 minutes, or until nicely browned and crisp on the outside.

2. Transfer to a plate. Open the sandwich and evenly spread the miso and garlic clove over the inside of one of the bread slices. Top with the fermented vegetables and lettuce, close the sandwich back up, cut in half, and serve immediately.

▶ **Variation Tip:** This concept also works for those who just want a plain ol' grilled cheese sandwich, like my daughter. I make her a version with only the vegan cheese (adding an extra slice to make up for the omitted toppings), and a little extra vegan butter on the outside of the bread.

Tamale Pie with Cilantro Lime Cornmeal Crust

FAMILY-FRIENDLY / GLUTEN-FREE / GREEN

<u>SERVES 4</u>

PREP TIME:
25 MINUTES

COOK TIME:
20 MINUTES

BAKE: 320°F

Per Serving:
Calories: 165;
Total fat: 5g;
Saturated fat: 1g;
Cholesterol: 0mg;
Sodium: 831mg;
Carbohydrates: 26g;
Fiber: 6g;
Protein: 6g

There's something so comforting and satisfying about this dish—perfect for evenings when you want to eat something that's both nutrient-dense and tasty. I spent years trying to recreate a frozen tamale pie I used to eat in the '90s, but I like this version even better! There's nothing like the combination of lime and cilantro to really kick up the volume. To make this dish for busy weeknights or larger crowds, prepare a double (or triple) batch of the filling (it'll store in the fridge for up to a week) and then when you're ready to go, make the cornmeal topping, assemble your pie, and pop it in the air fryer. If you like additional heat, you can also mince a jalapeño and add it to the cornmeal mixture. Also, please keep in mind that the "crust" has the consistency of polenta, not corn bread. I hope you love this one as much as I do—it's definitely a favorite in our house!

For the filling

1 medium zucchini, diced (1¼ cups)

2 teaspoons neutral-flavored oil (sunflower, safflower, or refined coconut)

1 cup cooked pinto beans, drained

1 cup canned diced tomatoes (unsalted) with juice

3 large garlic cloves, minced or pressed

1 tablespoon chickpea flour

1 teaspoon dried oregano

1 teaspoon onion granules

½ teaspoon salt

½ teaspoon crushed red chili flakes

Cooking oil spray (sunflower, safflower, or refined coconut)

For the crust

½ cup yellow cornmeal, finely ground

1½ cups water

½ teaspoon salt

1 teaspoon nutritional yeast

1 teaspoon neutral-flavored oil (sunflower, safflower, or refined coconut)

2 tablespoons finely chopped cilantro

½ teaspoon lime zest (see Cooking Tip on page 123)

To make the filling

1. In a large skillet set to medium-high heat, sauté the zucchini and oil for 3 minutes, or until the zucchini begins to brown.
2. Add the beans, tomatoes, garlic, flour, oregano, onion, salt, and chili flakes to the mixture. Cook over medium heat, stirring often, for 5 minutes, or until the mixture is thickened and no liquid remains. Remove from the heat.
3. Spray a 6-inch round, 2-inch deep baking pan with oil and place the mixture in the bottom. Smooth out the top and set aside.

To make the crust

1. In a medium pot over high heat, place the cornmeal, water, and salt. Whisk constantly as you bring the mixture to a boil. Once it boils, reduce the heat to very low. Add the nutritional yeast and oil and continue to cook, stirring very often, for 10 minutes or until the mixture is very thick and hard to whisk. Remove from the heat.
2. Stir the cilantro and lime zest into the cornmeal mixture until thoroughly combined. Using a rubber spatula, gently spread it evenly onto the filling in the baking pan to form a smooth crust topping. Place in the air fryer basket and bake for 20 minutes, or until the top is golden-brown. Let it cool for 5 to 10 minutes, then cut and serve.

Ginger Tahini Noodles
with Sesame Crunch Tofu

GLUTEN-FREE / BLUE

SERVES 3

PREP TIME:
20 TO
25 MINUTES

COOK TIME:
20 MINUTES

FRY: 392°F

Per Serving:
Calories: 549;
Total fat: 26g;
Saturated fat: 1g;
Cholesterol: 0mg;
Sodium: 1805mg;
Carbohydrates: 70g;
Fiber: 6g;
Protein: 8g

These delicious noodles are a ginger lover's delight and incredibly immune-boosting, with an extra hit of miso, lime, and garlic. Topped with the crunchy tofu, this satisfying array of flavors and textures is one of my go-to dishes. This recipe and the four that follow are some of my favorites for batch-cooking the tofu in advance. Briefly crisp it up in the air fryer before serving and get ready to enjoy a fresh, delicious, and easy meal.

Sesame Crunch Tofu (page 134)

1 (5.29-ounce) package bean thread noodles (3 "nests"; see Ingredient Tip on page 105)

3 tablespoons mellow white miso

3 tablespoons tahini (ground sesame paste)

3 tablespoons fresh lime juice

3 tablespoons grated fresh ginger

5 large garlic cloves, minced or pressed

1½ cups finely chopped cabbage (red or green, your choice)

1½ cups diced cucumber

½ cup chopped cilantro

⅓ cup finely chopped scallions

1. Prepare the Sesame Crunch Tofu.
2. While the tofu is cooking, you can get the rest of the dish together. Begin by cooking the noodles according to the directions on the package. (For bean threads, I bring water to a boil, add the nests so they're covered with the water, remove from heat and let sit, covered, for 5 minutes—or until the noodles are tender.)
3. In a large bowl, add the miso, tahini, and lime juice. Stir well to thoroughly combine, using a wire whisk or fork. Add the ginger and garlic and stir again.
4. Add the cabbage, cucumber, cilantro, and scallions to the bowl. Add the noodles to the bowl, and stir well. Serve topped with the tofu.

Asian Buffet Bowl with Crisp Tofu

FAMILY-FRIENDLY / GLUTEN-FREE / GREEN

SERVES 4

PREP TIME:
20 MINUTES
(including tofu
and sauce)

COOK TIME:
35 TO
37 MINUTES
(including rice,
tofu, and sauce)

FRY: 392°F

Per Serving:
Calories: 401;
Total fat: 12g;
Saturated fat: 3g;
Cholesterol: 0mg;
Sodium: 268mg;
Carbohydrates: 63g;
Fiber: 6g;
Protein: 14g

In our home, this is the ultimate family-friendly meal, because everyone gets to make up their own delicious bowl. We put all the toppings out on the counter so everyone can go down the line, choosing what they'd like. One thing I really love about this is that it seems to entice picky kids to make healthy choices. For cooked veggies, we especially like broccoli and snow peas; for raw veggies, we reach for julienned carrots, thinly sliced cucumbers, fresh cilantro, and minced scallions. Yum!

Double recipe of Crisp Tofu (page 132)

Asian Spicy Sweet Sauce (page 140)

4 cups cooked brown rice, brown rice noodles, or bean thread noodles

2 cups steamed, air-fried, or stir-fried vegetables, your choice

2 cups raw vegetables, cut thin, your choice

Toasted sesame seeds, for topping (optional)

Crushed peanuts (optional)

1. Make the Crisp Tofu. Remember to double it!
2. While that's cooking, prepare the Asian Spicy Sweet Sauce.
3. Place the rice or noodles, cooked vegetables, and raw veggie selections in individual bowls.
4. Once all of the components (including the tofu) are finished and in bowls, you're ready to party! For each serving, you will want to place some rice or noodles in the bottom of your bowl, top with vegetables, and then add the tofu, sauce, and any optional additions, if using. Dig in while still warm!

▶ **Variation Tip:** There are so many different ways to change this up! Feel free to use different proteins like Sesame Crunch Tofu (page 134) or Spicy Sweet Tempeh Cubes (page 136). You can also incorporate different sauces: Try some from the Panang Curry Bowl (page 100) or store-bought sweet chili sauce or sriracha if you're in a low-maintenance mood. And of course, feel free to vary the veggies.

Panang Curry Bowl

GLUTEN-FREE / PURPLE

SERVES 4

PREP TIME:
15 MINUTES

COOK TIME:
20 MINUTES
(plus time for rice
or noodles)

FRY: 392°F

Per Serving:
Calories: 894;
Total fat: 57g;
Saturated fat: 31g;
Cholesterol: 0mg;
Sodium: 1378mg;
Carbohydrates: 86g;
Fiber: 9g;
Protein: 16g

This "panang" is a shortcut version of the traditional Thai variety, but it's still scrumptious—plus, you can find all of the ingredients in any supermarket or health food store! I've left a lot of room in this recipe for customization, but here's my favorite way to enjoy this dish: I top brown rice (or noodles) with a combination of air-fried, steamed, and raw vegetables. Then I drizzle the sauce on top and add the tofu (I love both kinds of tofu, so I use whichever I'm in the mood for). My favorite steamed or air-fried vegetables for this dish include broccoli, cauliflower, and snow peas. For raw veggies, I love baby spinach, paper-thin cucumber, minced scallions, and finely chopped red cabbage. Have fun experimenting to find your favorite flavor combinations!

4 cups cooked rice or rice noodles, any variety

Sesame Crunch Tofu (page 134) or Crisp Tofu (page 132) (feel free to double the recipe)

1 (14-ounce) can full-fat coconut milk

¼ cup plus 2 tablespoons coconut sugar

¼ cup red curry paste

¼ cup natural peanut butter

2 tablespoons coconut oil

4 large garlic cloves, peeled

1 teaspoon sea salt

1 teaspoon grated lime zest

4 cups chopped vegetables, your choice

Sesame seeds, black or regular, for topping (optional)

1. If you haven't made the rice or noodles yet, you'll want to start them now, paying attention to what their cook time is in relation to the rest of the recipe.

2. Next, prepare the tofu of choice and begin cooking it in the air fryer, according to the recipe instructions.

3. While the tofu is cooking, make the sauce: In a blender jar, place the coconut milk, coconut sugar, red curry paste, peanut butter, coconut oil, garlic, salt, and lime zest and blend until very smooth. Set aside. (If you have leftovers—and you may—this will keep in an airtight container, refrigerated, for at least a week.)

4. Prepare your veggies (if using cauliflower and broccoli, air-fry for 5 to 8 minutes at 392° F) and set aside. Use the chart on page 144 to customize your veggie times.

5. When the tofu is close to being done, you may wish to gently heat the panang sauce over low heat on the stove, just until hot.

6. To serve: Place the cooked rice or noodles in your bowls, and top with the vegetables. Drizzle with a generous portion of sauce and top with tofu cubes. Sprinkle with sesame seeds, if using. Enjoy immediately.

Red Curry Noodles
with Sesame Crunch Tofu

GLUTEN-FREE / PURPLE

SERVES 4

PREP TIME:
20 MINUTES

COOK TIME:
20 MINUTES

FRY: 392°F

Per Serving:
Calories: 607;
Total fat: 40g;
Saturated fat: 27g;
Cholesterol: 0mg;
Sodium: 1256mg;
Carbohydrates: 59g;
Fiber: 6g;
Protein: 10g

If I even think about this dish, it creates a Pavlovian-like response in which my mouth begins to water. Dorky, but true. If you like full flavors as much as I do, these curry noodles might make you dork out too! I personally love the variety of textures and flavors here—it feels like a little food party. You've got the crispy tofu, paired with the saucy, tart noodles, and the crunch of fresh vegetables. Oh, and lest we forget, this dish is actually good for you, too! The immune-boosting properties of ginger, lime, and garlic are all present, along with antioxidant-rich fresh vegetables, which contain plenty of fresh enzymes and vitamins. You can also serve this with the Crisp Tofu (page 132) if you want to change things up, and double either tofu recipe if you'd like to increase the tofu-to-noodle ratio.

Sesame Crunch Tofu (page 134)

1 (8-ounce) package Thai rice noodles (preferably brown rice noodles)

2 tablespoons Thai red curry paste

1 (14-ounce) can full-fat coconut milk, divided

4 large garlic cloves, pressed or finely minced

2 tablespoons grated fresh ginger

¼ cup fresh lime juice

1 teaspoon sea salt

⅓ cup chopped cilantro

⅓ cup chopped fresh basil

⅓ cup minced scallions

⅓ cup finely chopped red cabbage

1. Prepare the Sesame Crunch Tofu.
2. While that's in the air fryer, get the rest of the dish together. Begin by cooking the noodles according to the directions on their package.
3. While the noodles are cooking, make the sauce: In a very large bowl, combine the curry paste and about ¼ cup of the coconut milk. Whisk together until smooth, using a wire whisk or fork. Add the remaining coconut milk and whisk again until emulsified. Add the garlic, ginger, lime juice, and salt. Stir or whisk well.

4. Add the cilantro, basil, scallions, and cabbage to the bowl and stir.
5. Once the noodles are al dente, drain thoroughly and add them to the bowl. Stir gently to thoroughly combine with the sauce. Serve the noodle-veggie mixture hot, topped with the Sesame Crunch Tofu.

▶ **Cooking Tip:** If you love this sauce and want more of it in your life, feel free to whip up a double batch and store the extra in the fridge. It can be used to jazz up brown rice or quinoa, steamed vegetables, or even as a dipping sauce for spring rolls.

Everyday Power Noodles

FAST / GLUTEN-FREE / GREEN

SERVES 3

PREP TIME:
10 MINUTES

COOK TIME:
15 MINUTES

FRY: 392°F

Per Serving:
Calories: 446;
Total fat: 12g;
Saturated fat: 2g;
Cholesterol: 0mg;
Sodium: 1698mg;
Carbohydrates: 74g;
Fiber: 9g;
Protein: 15g

Truth be told, this dish is an absolute go-to for me (I actually do eat it almost every day), and I normally make one-third of this recipe at a time, because I'm usually making it for lunch, just for myself. I love that it's easy to prepare, flavorful, immune-boosting, and contains three full cups of vegetables per serving! Miso has wonderful detoxifying properties, and shiitake mushrooms are highly renowned for their ability to stimulate the immune system. However, you're also welcome to change the veggies up—and I almost always do, depending on what I've got on hand. If you keep your vegetables chopped and ready to go in the fridge, this dish is especially easy to throw together. For an extra kick, top with some chili garlic sauce.

Crispy Salt and Pepper Tofu (page 74) or Crisp Tofu (page 132)

1 (5.29-ounce) package bean thread noodles (3 "nests")

1 tablespoon toasted sesame oil

3 tablespoons tamari or shoyu

2 cups shiitake mushroom caps, sliced

2 cups broccoli florets

4 large garlic cloves, minced or pressed

4 cups green cabbage

1 cup scallions, finely chopped

3 tablespoons miso (I use red miso, but any kind is fine)

1 tablespoon fresh lemon or lime juice

Bottled chili garlic sauce or sriracha (optional)

1. Prepare your tofu of choice according to the directions for its recipe.

2. While the tofu is air-frying, you'll be able to finish the rest of the dish: Begin by cooking the bean threads: Bring the water to a boil and add the bean thread nests so they're covered with the water. Remove from heat and let sit, covered, for 5 minutes—or until the noodles are tender. Drain and set aside.

3. While the bean threads are cooking, bring a large pan or wok to medium heat. Add the sesame oil, tamari, mushrooms, and broccoli. Stir-fry until the mushrooms are tender and the broccoli is bright green. Add the garlic, cabbage, and scallions and stir-fry for another minute, or until the cabbage is wilted. Remove from the heat.

4. In a small bowl, stir the miso and lemon or lime juice together until smooth. Add to the stir-fry mixture. Combine well. Add the bean thread noodles to the mixture and stir until well combined.

5. Serve immediately, topped with the tofu—and some of the chili garlic sauce or sriracha if you like.

▶ **Ingredient Tip:** *Bean thread noodles? What the heck are those?* Only my favorite kind of noodles! They can sometimes be tricky to find, but they're worth the effort. Also known as cellophane or glass noodles, bean thread noodles are made from mung bean starch and can be found in any Asian market, sometimes in health food stores, in the Asian section of supermarkets—and of course, online. I love them because they're quick and easy to cook: Just place in boiling water, let sit for 5 minutes, and drain! They magically come out perfect every time—unlike many other gluten-free noodles, these aren't mushy. Plus they have a cool, glass-like look to them. They are also relatively low in calories and portion-controlled. If you can't locate them, substitute with rice noodles, vermicelli, linguine, or spaghetti.

chapter 5

Desserts

"How Is This Vegan?"
Chocolate Cake
108

Chocolate Chip Cookies
110

Oatmeal Raisin Cookies
112

Easy Cinnamon Crisps
114

De-Light-Full
Caramelized Apples
115

Cozy Apple Crisp
116

Apple Puffs with
Vanilla Caramel Sauce
118

Strawberry Puffs with
Creamy Lemon Sauce
120

Gooey Lemon Bars
122

Raspberry Lemon
Streusel Cake
124

Pineapple
Upside-Down Cake
126

Blackberry
Peach Cobbler
128

◀ *Gooey Lemon Bars*

"How Is This Vegan?" Chocolate Cake

**FAMILY-FRIENDLY / GLUTEN-FREE
(WITH GLUTEN-FREE FLOUR) / PURPLE**

SERVES 6

PREP TIME:
10 MINUTES

COOK TIME:
25 MINUTES

BAKE: 347°F

Per Serving:
Calories: 341;
Total fat: 13g;
Saturated fat: 2g;
Cholesterol: 0mg;
Sodium: 280mg;
Carbohydrates: 56g;
Fiber: 4g;
Protein: 3g

Whenever I've made this dessert for omnivores, I'm invariably asked how it could possibly be vegan—hence, the name! Thus, it's a great dessert for those who may be skeptical of veganism, as well as anyone who just loves chocolate and wants some delicious cake in their life. It also makes a lovely birthday cake, especially if the birthday boy or girl doesn't necessarily want or need a standard-size cake. You can enjoy this cake plain, or top it with chocolate chips, cacao nibs, fresh berries, sprinkles, or anything else your heart desires.

For the cake

¾ cup flour (whole-wheat pastry, gluten-free all-purpose, or all-purpose)

½ cup organic sugar

2 tablespoons cocoa powder

½ teaspoon baking soda

⅛ teaspoon sea salt

½ cup nondairy milk

2½ tablespoons neutral flavored oil (sunflower, safflower, or melted refined coconut)

½ tablespoon apple cider vinegar

½ teaspoon vanilla

Coconut oil (for greasing)

For the frosting

3 tablespoons vegan margarine (Earth Balance sticks work well)

1¼ cups powdered sugar

5 tablespoons cocoa powder

2 teaspoons vanilla

⅛ teaspoon sea salt

To make the cake

1. In a medium bowl, using a wire whisk, stir together the flour, sugar, cocoa powder, baking soda, and salt. When thoroughly combined, add the milk, oil, vinegar, and vanilla. Stir just until well combined.

2. Preheat the air fryer for 2 minutes.

3. Grease a 6-inch round, 2-inch deep baking pan liberally with some coconut oil (this is important because you don't want the cake to stick to the pan). Pour the batter into the oiled pan and bake for 25 minutes, or until a knife inserted in the center comes out clean.

To make the frosting

1. In a medium bowl, using an electric beater, cream together the vegan margarine and powdered sugar. Add the cocoa powder, vanilla, and salt and whip with the beaters until thoroughly combined and fluffy. You'll probably want to scrape down the sides occasionally with a rubber spatula. Refrigerate until ready to use.

To assemble

1. Allow the cake to cool completely, and then run a knife around the edges of the baking pan. Turn it upside-down on a plate so it can be frosted on the sides and top.

2. Allow the cake to cool until no longer hot, usually about 10 minutes. When the frosting is no longer cold, use a butter knife or small spatula to frost the sides and top. Cut into slices and enjoy.

Chocolate Chip Cookies

**FAST / FAMILY-FRIENDLY / GLUTEN-FREE
(WITH GLUTEN-FREE FLOUR) / BLUE**

**MAKES
6 COOKIES**

PREP TIME:
10 MINUTES

COOK TIME:
7 MINUTES

BAKE: 347°F

Per Serving:
Calories: 71;
Total fat: 3g;
Saturated fat: 2g;
Cholesterol: 0mg;
Sodium: 81mg;
Carbohydrates: 11g;
Fiber: 1g;
Protein: 1g

Oh, darling chocolate chip cookie, how I love thee! When I gave up refined sugar years ago, I stopped eating cookies, because I thought they only existed in the land of white sugar. However, since then, I've found that coconut sugar is a wonderful low-glycemic sweetener that works nicely here (and in most recipes), and even gives a rich depth of flavor as a bonus! There are also stevia-sweetened chocolate chips you can use if you're like me and want to keep refined sugars to a minimum (my favorite brand is Lily's). Of course, if you don't care about all of that, use any chocolate chips you like, or even break apart a great dark chocolate bar (the brand Hu makes gorgeous organic vegan chocolate bars, sweetened only with coconut sugar—if you really want to take things to the next level, use one of their salted chocolate bars) and make these into "chocolate chunk" cookies!

1 tablespoon refined coconut oil, melted

1 tablespoon maple syrup

1 tablespoon nondairy milk

½ teaspoon vanilla

¼ cup plus 2 tablespoons whole-wheat pastry flour or all-purpose gluten-free flour

2 tablespoons coconut sugar

¼ teaspoon sea salt

¼ teaspoon baking powder

2 tablespoons vegan chocolate chips

Cooking oil spray (sunflower, safflower, or refined coconut)

1. In a medium bowl, stir together the oil, maple syrup, milk, and vanilla. Add the flour, coconut sugar, salt, and baking powder. Stir just until thoroughly combined. Stir in the chocolate chips.
2. Preheat the air fryer basket (with a 6-inch round, 2-inch deep baking pan inside) for 2 minutes. Then, spray the pan lightly with oil. Drop tablespoonfuls of the batter onto the pan, leaving a little room in between in case they spread out a bit. Bake for 7 minutes, or until lightly browned. Be careful not to overcook.
3. Gently transfer to a cooling rack (or plate). Repeat as desired, making

all of the cookies at once, or keeping the batter on hand in the fridge to be used later (it will keep refrigerated in an airtight container for about a week). Enjoy warm if possible!

▶ **Cooking Tip:** These are my "safe" chocolate chip cookies, because even if I eat the whole batch over the course of a day or two, I don't feel too horrible about it. Of course, if you have tons of self-control around warm, gooey cookies (are you even human?), feel free to double or triple the batch. However, I personally enjoy keeping the batter on hand in the fridge so I can make up just a few when I need cookie love.

Oatmeal Raisin Cookies

**FAST / FAMILY-FRIENDLY / GLUTEN-FREE
(WITH GLUTEN-FREE FLOUR) / PURPLE**

**MAKES ABOUT
18 COOKIES**

PREP TIME:
10 MINUTES

COOK TIME:
7 MINUTES

BAKE: 347°F

Per Serving:
Calories: 78;
Total fat: 4g;
Saturated fat: 1g;
Cholesterol: 0mg;
Sodium: 82mg;
Carbohydrates: 11g;
Fiber: 1g;
Protein: 1g

You know what's really great about cookies in the air fryer? You can keep the batter on hand in the fridge and "bake" warm cookies at a moment's notice, without having to heat up an entire oven or wash a huge cookie sheet. If you're really an oatmeal cookie lover, you can also double this recipe so you'll have more batter on hand for future happiness. And yes, raisin haters, you can leave them out or substitute chocolate chips (or another variety of dried fruit) here. However, for those of us who don't hate raisins, there's something just so right about the combination of oatmeal and raisins, especially in a warm, freshly baked cookie.

¼ cup plus ½ tablespoon vegan margarine

2½ tablespoons nondairy milk, plain and unsweetened

½ cup organic sugar

½ teaspoon vanilla extract

½ teaspoon plus ⅛ teaspoon ground cinnamon

½ cup plus 2 tablespoons flour (whole-wheat pastry,

gluten-free all-purpose, or all-purpose)

¼ teaspoon sea salt

¾ cup rolled oats

¼ teaspoon baking soda

¼ teaspoon baking powder

2 tablespoons raisins

Cooking oil spray (sunflower, safflower, or refined coconut)

1. In a medium bowl, using an electric beater, whip the margarine until fluffy.

2. Add in the milk, sugar, and vanilla. Stir or whip with beaters until well combined.

3. In a separate bowl, add the cinnamon, flour, salt, oats, baking soda, and baking powder and stir well to combine. Add the dry mixture to the wet mixture and combine everything well with a wooden spoon. Stir in the raisins.

4. Preheat the air fryer basket (with your 6-inch round, 2-inch deep baking pan inside) for 2 minutes. Then, spray the pan lightly with oil. Drop tablespoonfuls of the batter onto the pan, leaving a little room in between each one as they'll probably spread out a bit. Bake for about 7 minutes, or until lightly browned.

5. Gently transfer to a cooling rack (or plate), being careful to leave the cookies intact. Repeat as desired, making all of the cookies at once, or keeping the batter on hand in the fridge to be used later (it will keep refrigerated in an airtight container for a week to 10 days).

▶ **Substitution Tip:** You may substitute coconut oil for the margarine if you prefer. However, if you do this, add a pinch more salt, as the oil will be salt-free, unlike the margarine. Also, if you do use the vegan margarine as directed, keep in mind that the "pure fat" variety will work best (as opposed to the whipped, lower-fat variety). Finally, if you're trying to reduce the fat overall, applesauce can be substituted for part of the fat in these cookies, although I wouldn't substitute it entirely, as the results can be overly sweet and a bit dry.

Easy Cinnamon Crisps

FAST / FAMILY-FRIENDLY / GREEN

SERVES 4

PREP TIME:
2 MINUTES

COOK TIME:
5 TO 6 MINUTES

FRY: 347°F

Per Serving:
Calories: 45;
Total fat: 1g;
Saturated fat: 0g;
Cholesterol: 0mg;
Sodium: 73mg;
Carbohydrates: 8g;
Fiber: 1g;
Protein: 1g

This is the ultimate quick-and-easy dessert! It's just a matter of cut, sprinkle, spray, and air-fry. I also love that it can be a healthy treat as well—just by using a sprouted whole grain (or gluten-free brown rice) tortilla, you'll be getting lots of fiber and nutrients, and a healthy serving of complex carbs. Plus, with only coconut sugar to sweeten these crisps, you'll have a higher-nutrient, lower-glycemic sweet treat you can feel good about. One thing to note: In a cooking class where I served these, everyone agreed the crisps were much better when both sides were sprayed with a little oil—it keeps them from being dry, and gives them that satisfying "fried" crunch.

1 (8-inch) tortilla, preferably sprouted whole-grain

Cooking oil spray (sunflower, safflower, or refined coconut)

2 teaspoons coconut sugar

½ teaspoon cinnamon

1. Cut the tortilla into 8 triangles (like a pizza). Place on a large plate and spray both sides with oil.
2. Sprinkle the tops evenly with the coconut sugar and cinnamon. In short spurts, spray the tops again with the oil. (If you spray too hard for this step, it will make the powdery toppings fly off!)
3. Place directly in the air fryer basket in a single layer (it's okay if they overlap a little, but do your best to give them space). Fry for 5 to 6 minutes, or until the triangles are lightly browned, but not *too* brown—they're bitter if overcooked. Enjoy warm if possible.

De-Light-Full Caramelized Apples

FAST / FAMILY-FRIENDLY / GLUTEN-FREE / GREEN

SERVES 2

PREP TIME:
4 MINUTES

COOK TIME:
20 MINUTES

BAKE: 392°F

Per Serving:
Calories: 120;
Total fat: 1g;
Saturated fat: 0g;
Cholesterol: 0mg;
Sodium: 113mg;
Carbohydrates: 33g;
Fiber: 6g;
Protein: 1g

Where do I even begin with this one? For starters, here's a dessert that's basically as light and wholesome as a gosh-darned apple, yet gives you the feel of eating warm, gooey comfort food. Oh, and another thing—these are so, so easy to make! You cut an apple, sprinkle it with a couple of things, and bake it in the air fryer. Boom. Once cooked, you can serve these plain, or top them with Gorgeous Granola (page 20) or a lil' scoop of vegan vanilla ice cream. On a personal note, I particularly love this dish because my sweet grandma (oh, I miss her so) used to make baked apples for me on cold winter nights. To me, it always felt like love on a plate—and I hope it evokes a wonderful, warm-fuzzy feeling for you, too.

2 apples, any sweet variety

2 tablespoons water

1½ teaspoons coconut sugar

¼ teaspoon cinnamon

Pinch nutmeg

Dash sea salt

Cooking oil spray (sunflower, safflower, or refined coconut)

1. Cut each apple in half (no need to peel) and then remove the core and seeds, doing your best to keep the apple halves intact—because ideally, you want apple halves, not quarters.

2. Place the apples upright in a 6-inch round, 2-inch deep baking pan. Add about 2 tablespoons water to the bottom of the dish to keep the apples from drying out (the apples will sit in the water).

3. Sprinkle the tops of the apples evenly with the sugar, cinnamon, and nutmeg. Give each half a very light sprinkle of sea salt.

4. In short spurts, spray the tops with oil (if you spray too hard, it will make the toppings fly off in a tragic whirlwind). Once moistened, spray the tops again with oil. (This will keep them from drying out.)

5. Bake for 20 minutes, or until the apples are very soft and nicely browned on top. Enjoy immediately, plain or topped with granola and/or ice cream.

Cozy Apple Crisp

FAMILY-FRIENDLY / GLUTEN-FREE (WITH GLUTEN-FREE FLOUR) / BLUE

SERVES 4

PREP TIME:
10 MINUTES

COOK TIME:
30 MINUTES

BAKE: 320°F

Per Serving:
Calories: 172;
Total fat: 7g;
Saturated fat: 6g;
Cholesterol: 0mg;
Sodium: 59mg;
Carbohydrates: 29g;
Fiber: 4g;
Protein: 1g

This dessert feels timeless to me—it's my version of the apple crisp recipe my grandmother handed down to me, which was handed down to her from her aunt (whom we all referred to as "Grandma Clark"). I made it vegan (and considerably healthier) by reducing the fat and sugar and replacing the animal products with plant-based alternatives. I have such happy memories of eating this by the fireplace with my grandma, as it was something she made on a fairly regular basis. She'd serve it fresh out of the oven, topped with a little milk—of course, once I went vegan, I'd use nondairy milk. If that's not your cup of tea (or milk, in this case), this is also delicious plain or with a scoop of vegan vanilla ice cream.

For the topping

2 tablespoons coconut oil

¼ cup plus 2 tablespoons whole-wheat pastry flour (or gluten-free all-purpose flour)

¼ cup coconut sugar

⅛ teaspoon sea salt

For the filling

2 cups finely chopped (or thinly sliced) apples (no need to peel)

3 tablespoons water

½ tablespoon lemon juice

¾ teaspoon cinnamon

To make the topping

In a bowl, combine the oil, flour, sugar, and salt. Mix the ingredients together thoroughly, either with your hands or a spoon. The mixture should be crumbly; if it's not, place it in the fridge until it solidifies a bit.

To make the filling

1. In a 6-inch round, 2-inch deep baking pan, stir the apples with the water, lemon juice, and cinnamon until well combined.

2. Crumble the chilled topping over the apples. Bake for 30 minutes, or until the apples are tender and the crumble is crunchy and nicely browned. Serve immediately on its own or topped with nondairy milk, vegan ice cream, or nondairy whipped cream.

▷ **Variation Tip:** My daughter and I both love this dessert, but disagree on what constitutes the best crumble topping. I prefer the one that's written in the recipe, above. However, she prefers a more decadent version that includes vegan margarine and regular sugar. If you'd like to try her version (and she strongly suggests you do), simply replace the coconut oil with vegan margarine and the coconut sugar with organic white sugar.

▷ **Ingredient Tip:** I'm often asked what type of apples work best in this recipe. And in all honesty, I don't have an impressive answer—I tend to just search out the best-looking organic apples at the store. As long as they're not overly tart, most varieties will work wonderfully.

Apple Puffs with Vanilla Caramel Sauce

FAST / FAMILY-FRIENDLY / PURPLE

MAKES 6 PUFFS

PREP TIME:
20 MINUTES

COOK TIME:
10 MINUTES

BAKE: 320°F

Per Serving:
Calories: 366;
Total fat: 16g;
Saturated fat: 12g;
Cholesterol: 0mg;
Sodium: 296mg;
Carbohydrates: 58g;
Fiber: 3g;
Protein: 2g

This dessert will impress even the pickiest of guests, yet comes together in less than half an hour! I have a vivid memory of making this for a cooking class, and almost every student licked (yes, licked) their plate. No, they weren't barbarians—the sauce is just that good. You may also notice that it calls for a real, live vanilla bean. Please don't be intimidated by that! Yes, finding intact vanilla beans takes a little work (and aren't always cheap), but they're absolutely worth it. There's nothing like the flavor of fresh vanilla. You can find them in any health food store and in most supermarkets. However, if you'd rather throw caution to the wind and avoid the vanilla bean quest altogether, you may substitute a tablespoon of vanilla extract.

For the filling

- 2 medium apples, cored and finely diced (no need to peel)
- 2 teaspoons cinnamon
- 2 tablespoons coconut sugar
- ⅛ teaspoon sea salt
- Cooking oil spray (sunflower, safflower, or refined coconut)
- 6 large (13-inch x 17-inch) sheets of phyllo dough, thawed (see Ingredient Tip)

For the vanilla caramel sauce

- 6-inch segment of a vanilla bean
- ½ cup plus 1 tablespoon maple syrup
- ¼ cup plus 2 tablespoons refined coconut oil (or vegan margarine)
- ¼ cup coconut sugar
- ½ teaspoon sea salt

To make the filling

1. In a medium bowl, combine the apples, cinnamon, coconut sugar, and salt and set aside.
2. Spray the air fryer basket with oil and set aside. Gently unwrap the phyllo dough. Remove 6 sheets and carefully set them aside. Wrap the remaining phyllo in airtight plastic wrap and place back in the fridge.

To assemble the puffs

1. Remove 1 large sheet of phyllo and place on a clean, dry surface. Spray with the oil. Fold it into thirds (the long way, so that you form a long,

skinny rectangle). As you go, spray each portion of dry phyllo, so the exposed phyllo continually gets lightly coated with oil—this will give you a more flaky (vs. dry) result.

2. Place ⅓ cup of the apple mixture at the base of the phyllo rectangle. Fold the bottom of the phyllo up and over the mixture. Continue to fold up toward the top, forming it into a triangle as you go. Once you have an apple-filled triangle, place it in the air fryer basket and spray the top with oil.

3. Repeat with the remaining phyllo and apple mixture. Note: You'll probably only be able to fit 3 puffs in your air fryer at a time, because you don't want them to overlap. If you don't wish to make a second batch right now, store the phyllo-wrapped, uncooked puffs in an airtight container in the fridge and air-fry them within a day or two.

4. Bake for 10 minutes, or until very golden-browned.

To make the sauce

1. Make a lengthwise cut all the way down the vanilla bean with a sharp knife and pry it open. Scrape out the insides with a table knife and place in a small pot. Add the maple syrup, oil, coconut sugar, and salt to the pot and set to medium-low heat, stirring very well to combine. After the sauce comes to a boil, reduce the heat to low and simmer gently for 3 to 5 minutes, or until slightly thickened.

2. Transfer the apple puffs to a plate and top with the caramel sauce. Enjoy while warm.

▶ **Ingredient Tip:** Phyllo (aka filo) dough is really easy to use, so don't be intimidated! There are just a few things you need to know: First, be sure to thaw frozen packages in the fridge overnight. I don't find it necessary to cover the unwrapped dough with damp towels, as most recipes suggest—just have the filling ready to go, and then work quickly once you've opened the package. And of course, be very gentle when working with phyllo, as it tears easily—but if it does tear, just place another sheet on top (or "patch" it with additional phyllo), and no one will ever know!

Strawberry Puffs with Creamy Lemon Sauce

FAST / FAMILY-FRIENDLY / PURPLE

MAKES 8 PUFFS

PREP TIME:
20 MINUTES

COOK TIME:
10 MINUTES

BAKE: 320°F

Per Serving:
Calories: 295;
Total fat: 14g;
Saturated fat: 2g;
Cholesterol: 0mg;
Sodium: 199mg;
Carbohydrates: 38g;
Fiber: 2g;
Protein: 6g

Phyllo treats are such a great way to wow your guests with minimal effort (shhh—this can be our little secret). This recipe is free from refined sugars, because I prefer to avoid them (and because the nutrient-rich Creamy Lemon Sauce is completely scrumptious without!). However, if you prefer a simpler finish to these puffs, just dust them with powdered sugar and top with fresh strawberry slices. If you're like me and adore the sauce, make a double batch—it's also delicious with the Pineapple Upside-Down Cake (page 126). Please refer to the Cooking Tip, as you'll need to plan ahead if you don't have a high-speed blender.

For the filling

- 3 cups sliced strawberries, fresh or frozen (1½ pints or 24 ounces)
- 1 cup sugar-free strawberry jam (sweetened only with fruit juice)
- 1 tablespoon arrowroot (or cornstarch)
- Cooking oil spray (sunflower, safflower, or refined coconut)
- 8 large (13-inch x 17-inch) sheets of phyllo dough, thawed (see Ingredient Tip on page 119)

For the sauce

- 1 cup raw cashew pieces (see Cooking Tip)
- ¼ cup plus 2 tablespoons raw agave nectar
- ¼ cup plus 1 tablespoon water
- 3 tablespoons fresh lemon juice
- 2 teaspoons (packed) lemon zest (see Cooking Tip on page 123)
- 2 tablespoons neutral-flavored oil (sunflower, safflower, or refined coconut)
- 2 teaspoons vanilla
- ¼ teaspoon sea salt

To make the filling

1. In a medium bowl, add the strawberries, jam, and arrowroot and stir well to combine. Set aside.
2. Spray the air fryer basket with oil and set aside.

To assemble the puffs

1. Gently unwrap the phyllo dough. Remove 8 sheets and carefully set them aside. Re-wrap the remaining phyllo in airtight plastic wrap and place back in the fridge.

2. Remove 1 large sheet of phyllo and place on a clean, dry surface. Spray with the oil. Fold it into thirds so that it forms a long, skinny rectangle. As you go, spray each portion of dry phyllo, so the exposed phyllo continually gets lightly coated with oil.

3. Place about ⅓ cup of the strawberry mixture at the base of the phyllo rectangle. Fold the bottom of the phyllo up and over the mixture. Continue to fold up toward the top, forming it into a triangle as you go. Once fully wrapped, place it in the air fryer basket and spray the top with oil.

4. Repeat with the remaining phyllo and strawberry mixture. Note you'll probably only be able to fit 3 puffs in your air fryer at a time, because you don't want them to overlap.

5. Bake for 10 minutes, or until beautifully golden-browned.

To make the sauce

1. Place the cashews, agave, water, lemon juice and zest, oil, vanilla, and salt in a blender. Process until completely smooth and velvety. (Any leftover sauce will keep nicely in the fridge for up to a week.)

2. Transfer the strawberry puffs to a plate and drizzle with the creamy lemon sauce. If desired, garnish with sliced strawberries. Enjoy while warm.

▶ **Cooking Tip:** If your blender isn't a high-speed one (such as Vitamix or Blendtec), you'll need to soak the cashews in enough water to cover them for several hours so they'll be soft enough to blend. Then simply drain off the water. Even those of us with high-speed blenders should take care to scrape down the sides and blend very thoroughly, in order to achieve an ultra-smooth, non-grainy result.

Gooey Lemon Bars

FAMILY-FRIENDLY / PURPLE

SERVES 6

PREP TIME:
15 MINUTES

COOK TIME:
25 MINUTES

BAKE: 347°F

Per Serving:
Calories: 202;
Total fat: 9g;
Saturated fat: 8g;
Cholesterol: 0mg;
Sodium: 3mg; Car-
bohydrates: 30g;
Fiber: 2g;
Protein: 1g

Ooey, gooey delicious! These dangerously delectable treats come together quickly to create a lemon lover's dream dessert. If you don't love lemon, this probably isn't the dish for you—I purposely created these with a serious kick, because I can't be bothered with a paltry "hint of lemon" when it comes to lemony desserts. Incidentally, these are one of my daughter's all-time favorite treats. She's requested them over cake for quite a few birthday parties over the years! There's something unbeatable about the combination of lemony tartness with just the right amount of sweetness.

For the crust

¾ **cup whole-wheat pastry flour**

2 **tablespoons powdered sugar**

¼ **cup refined coconut oil, melted**

For the filling

½ **cup organic sugar**

1 **packed tablespoon lemon zest (see Cooking Tip)**

¼ **cup fresh lemon juice**

⅛ **teaspoon sea salt**

¼ **cup unsweetened, plain applesauce**

1¾ **teaspoons arrowroot (or cornstarch)**

¾ **teaspoon baking powder**

Cooking oil spray (sunflower, safflower, or refined coconut)

To make the crust

In a small bowl, stir the flour, powdered sugar, and oil together just until well combined. Place in the fridge.

To make the filling

In a medium bowl, add the sugar, lemon zest and juice, salt, applesauce, arrowroot, and baking powder. Stir well.

To assemble the bars

1. Spray a 6-inch round, 2-inch deep baking pan lightly with oil. Remove the crust mixture from the fridge and gently press it into the bottom of the pan to form a crust. Place in the air fryer and bake for 5 minutes, or until it becomes slightly firm to the touch.

2. Remove and spread the lemon filling over the crust. Bake for about 18 to 20 minutes, or until the top is nicely browned. Remove and allow to cool for an hour or more in the fridge. Once firm and cooled, cut into pieces and serve. You might use a fork to get each piece out, as the pan is a little small for traditional spatulas.

▷ **Cooking Tip:** Don't let the idea of zesting a lemon scare you away if it's new to you! All you'll need is a fine grater or Microplane. The most important thing to remember is to gently zest *only* the yellow outer peel of the lemon, because if you zest the white parts beneath that, it will taste bitter—and you're going for tart, not bitter. This tip applies to zesting limes and oranges as well, and once you get the hang of it, you'll find citrus zest adds a pop of flavor to a wide range of dishes!

Raspberry Lemon Streusel Cake

**FAMILY-FRIENDLY / GLUTEN-FREE
(WITH GLUTEN-FREE FLOUR) / PURPLE**

SERVES 6

PREP TIME:
15 MINUTES

COOK TIME:
45 MINUTES

BAKE: 311°F

Per Serving:
Calories: 296;
Total fat: 11g;
Saturated fat: 1g;
Cholesterol: 0mg;
Sodium: 152mg;
Carbohydrates: 49g;
Fiber: 4g;
Protein: 3g

Lemon and raspberries are one of food's most perfect marriages, according to my daughter. She loves them together in pancakes, muffins, and especially this cake. In fact, she's one of my very best taste testers. That kid has one heck of a refined palate! Her comment upon my first efforts of this recipe were, "Very good, but could use more lemon." Hence, the extra zest in the frosting in order to give it a bit more pop. Of course, if you're not a lemon lover, you can reduce the amount of zest used here. (For tips on zesting citrus, please refer to the Cooking Tip on page 123.) And as with most baked goods, if you're gluten-free, you can try an all-purpose gluten-free flour here instead of the whole-wheat. Incidentally, this was a favorite recipe among my recipe testers!

For the streusel topping

2 tablespoons organic sugar

2 tablespoons neutral-flavored oil (sunflower, safflower, or refined coconut)

¼ cup plus 2 tablespoons whole-wheat pastry flour (or gluten-free all-purpose flour)

For the cake

1 cup whole-wheat pastry flour

½ cup organic sugar

1 teaspoon baking powder

1 tablespoon lemon zest

¼ teaspoon sea salt

¾ cup plus 2 tablespoons unsweetened nondairy milk (plain or vanilla)

2 tablespoons neutral-flavored oil (sunflower, safflower, or refined coconut)

1 teaspoon vanilla

1 cup fresh raspberries

Cooking oil spray (sunflower, safflower, or refined coconut)

For the icing

½ cup powdered sugar

1 tablespoon fresh lemon juice

½ teaspoon lemon zest

½ teaspoon vanilla

⅛ teaspoon sea salt

To make the streusel

In a small bowl, stir together the sugar, oil, and flour and place in the refrigerator (this will help it firm up and be more crumbly later).

To make the cake

1. In a medium bowl, place the flour, sugar, baking powder, zest, and salt. Stir very well, preferably with a wire whisk. Add the milk, oil, and vanilla. Stir with a rubber spatula or spoon, just until thoroughly combined. Gently stir in the raspberries.
2. Preheat the air fryer for 3 minutes. Spray or coat the insides of a 6-inch round, 2-inch deep baking pan with oil and pour the batter into the pan.
3. Remove the streusel from the fridge and crumble it over the top of the cake batter. Carefully place the cake in the air fryer and bake for 45 minutes, or until a knife inserted in the center comes out clean (the top should be golden-brown).

To make the icing

In a small bowl, stir together the powdered sugar, lemon juice and zest, vanilla, and salt. Once the cake has cooled for about 5 minutes, slice into 4 pieces and drizzle each with icing. Serve warm if possible. If you have leftovers, they will keep in an airtight container in the fridge for several days.

Pineapple Upside-Down Cake

FAMILY-FRIENDLY / BLUE

SERVES 6

PREP TIME:
10 MINUTES

COOK TIME:
30 MINUTES

BAKE: 320°F

Per Serving:
Calories: 191;
Total fat: 5g;
Saturated fat: 4g;
Cholesterol: 0mg;
Sodium: 183mg;
Carbohydrates: 35g;
Fiber: 4g;
Protein: 2g

This simple cake takes me back to the pineapple upside-down cakes from my childhood—there's something so comforting and familiar about these flavors! This version is much lighter and healthier, and especially good with the Creamy Lemon Sauce or vegan ice cream (I recommend NadaMoo's vanilla or Coconut Bliss's Naked Coconut). The easiest way to approach the pineapple juice and rings in this recipe is to buy a can of pineapple rings in their own juice and then use the amounts directed in the recipe. You'll have some leftovers, but you can pop those into the fridge (or freezer) for future use. As this cake contains less oil than typical baked goods, it can become a smidge dry when left over—so if at all possible, serve it when it's freshly made and warm.

1 cup whole-wheat pastry flour

1½ tablespoons ground flaxseed

½ teaspoon plus ⅛ teaspoon baking soda

¼ teaspoon sea salt

½ cup pineapple juice, fresh or canned

2 tablespoons melted coconut oil (plus more for greasing your pan)

¼ cup plus 2 tablespoons agave nectar

½ tablespoon fresh lemon juice

1 teaspoon vanilla

1 to 2 tablespoons coconut sugar (for coating the pan)

3 pineapple rings (fresh or canned)

Creamy Lemon Sauce (page 120) (optional)

Vanilla or coconut vegan ice cream (optional)

Vegan whipped topping (optional)

1. In a medium bowl, add the flour, flaxmeal, baking soda, and salt. Whisk very well. Add the pineapple juice, oil, agave, lemon juice, and vanilla. Stir just until thoroughly combined.

2. Preheat your air fryer for 2 minutes. Generously grease the bottom and sides of a 6-inch round, 2-inch deep baking pan with coconut oil. Sprinkle the bottom of the pan evenly with the coconut sugar (just enough to lightly coat the bottom of your pan).

3. Place the pineapple rings on top of the sugar in a single layer (you may need to break up some of the rings to do this). Pour the batter on top of the pineapple rings.

4. Carefully place the pan into your preheated air fryer. Bake for 25 to 30 minutes, or until a knife inserted into the center comes out clean. Note: Your cake may look done before the center is actually cooked through, so the knife test is where it's at here.

5. Carefully remove the pan and allow to cool on a plate or wire rack for 3 to 5 minutes. Run a knife around the edges of the pan. Place a plate on top (so that the plate is against the exposed cake). Gently flip over, so the cake is upside-down on the plate. Next, gently pull the baking pan off the cake so that the pineapple rings remain on top. Cut and serve—plain, or with Creamy Lemon Sauce, vegan ice cream, or whipped topping.

Blackberry Peach Cobbler

FAST / FAMILY-FRIENDLY / BLUE

SERVES 4

PREP TIME:
10 MINUTES

COOK TIME:
20 MINUTES

BAKE: 320°F

Per Serving:
Calories: 248;
Total fat: 8g;
Saturated fat: 1g;
Cholesterol: 0mg;
Sodium: 61mg;
Carbohydrates: 42g;
Fiber: 6g;
Protein: 3g

There's something so comforting and lovely about a good cobbler—the combination of gooey, warm fruit with a crunchy and lightly sweet topping just sends me. If you want to take this up a notch, serve with a vegan whipped cream or vanilla ice cream (I love the NadaMoo vanilla ice cream, but any kind will do—this cobbler would also be great with coconut or another favorite flavor). You can also experiment with different fruits in the filling. For example, my daughter loves this with raspberries or blueberries, especially when they're in season. Also try combining blueberries with peaches in high summer or apples and figs in the fall.

For the filling

1½ cups chopped peaches
(cut into ½-inch thick pieces)

1 (6-ounce) package
blackberries

2 tablespoons coconut sugar

2 teaspoons arrowroot
(or cornstarch)

1 teaspoon lemon juice

For the topping

2 tablespoons neutral-flavored
oil (sunflower, safflower,
or refined coconut)

1 tablespoon maple syrup

1 teaspoon vanilla

½ cup rolled oats

⅓ cup whole-wheat pastry
flour

3 tablespoons coconut
sugar

1 teaspoon cinnamon

¼ teaspoon nutmeg

⅛ teaspoon sea salt

To make the filling

In a 6-inch round, 2-inch deep baking pan, place the peaches, blackberries, coconut sugar, arrowroot, and lemon juice. Stir well with a rubber spatula, until thoroughly combined. Set aside.

To make the topping

1. In a separate bowl, combine the oil, maple syrup, and vanilla. Stir well. Add the oats, flour, coconut sugar, cinnamon, nutmeg, and salt. Stir well, until thoroughly combined. Crumble evenly over the peach-blackberry filling.

2. Bake for 20 minutes, or until the topping is crisp and lightly browned. Enjoy warm if at all possible, because it's beyond wonderful that way!

▷ **Ingredient Tip:** The sweetness level of peaches can vary so much! If you're using peaches that are very ripe and sweet, you may not need as much coconut sugar. You can also substitute frozen peaches here, as it's not always easy to find them fresh unless they're in season. One 10-ounce bag of frozen peaches is what you'll need for this recipe, but make sure to thaw and chop them before using them.

chapter 6

Staples

Crisp Tofu

132

Sesame Crunch Tofu

134

Zen Tofu

135

Spicy Sweet Tempeh Cubes

136

Cheesy Sauce

138

Asian Spicy Sweet Sauce

140

No-Dairy Ranch Dressing

141

Green Chili Sauce

142

Cilantro Chutney

143

◀ *Cilantro Chutney*

Crisp Tofu

FAST / FAMILY-FRIENDLY / GLUTEN-FREE / GREEN

SERVES 3

PREP TIME:
2 MINUTES

COOK TIME:
16 MINUTES

FRY: 392°F

Per Serving:
Calories: 81;
Total fat: 6g;
Saturated fat: 1g;
Cholesterol: 0mg;
Sodium: 165mg;
Carbohydrates: 1g;
Fiber: 1g;
Protein: 6g

Have you ever been to a Thai restaurant and ordered "Tofu Tod," the deep-fried crispy tofu appetizer? It doesn't have a lot of flavor, but it somehow works—the crisp exterior paired with the pillowy interior is so satisfying. I'm quite familiar with this dish because my daughter is slightly obsessed—once she ordered two plates of it instead of an entrée! That's the kind of tofu I was going for here, but I like the air-fried version even better. Not only is it healthier, it's crispier. Enjoy this tofu on its own or with Asian Spicy Sweet Sauce (page 140) or your favorite peanut sauce. It's also great as a topping for stir-fries, noodle dishes, or salads. And if you prefer an even quicker, lighter version, skip the 2 teaspoons of oil and instead just spritz the tofu with oil twice—once when it goes in the basket, and then again after you flip it.

1 (8-ounce) package tofu, firm or extra-firm (see Ingredient Tip)

2 teaspoons neutral-flavored oil (such as refined coconut, sunflower, or safflower), divided

Cooking oil spray (sunflower, safflower, or refined coconut)

¼ teaspoon sea salt

1. Cut the tofu into ½-inch thick slabs (no need to press the tofu for this recipe). Next, cut the slabs into triangles, roughly 1 inch in size.

2. In a medium bowl, toss the tofu gently with 1 teaspoon oil. Spray your air fryer basket with the oil spray. Place the tofu in the air fryer basket and fry for 8 minutes, setting the bowl aside for future use.

3. Remove the tofu, place back in the bowl, and toss gently with the remaining oil and the salt, using a rubber spatula so the tofu is thoroughly coated. Place the tofu back in the air fryer basket and fry for 8 minutes, until the tofu is golden-brown and crisp. Enjoy while warm.

▶ **Ingredient Tip:** When choosing a tofu for any savory application, you'll generally want a water-packed firm or extra-firm variety. I personally love the sprouted tofu that's available in most stores, because it's higher in nutrients, and tastes even more bright and fresh. You may find it helps to experiment with a few different brands and varieties until you find your favorite. Keep in mind that silken tofu has a very different texture, which is ideal for smooth-textured desserts such as the cream sauce in the Strawberry Delight Breakfast Parfail (page 21), but not for most savory applications. Silken tofu is sold in aseptic packs, and isn't refrigerated, unlike the water-packed, refrigerated variety I call for in this recipe.

Sesame Crunch Tofu

FAST / FAMILY-FRIENDLY / GLUTEN-FREE (WITH GLUTEN-FREE FLOUR) / BLUE

SERVES 3

PREP TIME:
10 MINUTES

COOK TIME:
20 MINUTES

BAKE: 392°F

Per Serving:
Calories: 183;
Total fat: 18g;
Saturated fat: 2g;
Cholesterol: 0mg;
Sodium: 505mg;
Carbohydrates: 5g;
Fiber: 2g;
Protein: 4g

In our household, here's how the conversation goes: I ask my daughter if she wants some tofu. She says, "What kind are you making?" If I answer anything other than "Sesame tofu," she'll usually respond, "No, thanks. I'm not hungry." But it's not just my girl who adores this—I've never met a person (even self-confirmed tofu haters and picky kids) who didn't love this dish. You can eat it plain, or as a topping for stir-fries, bowls, or salads. It also makes a scrumptious stand-alone appetizer when served with the Asian Spicy Sweet Sauce (page 140) for dipping.

1 (8-ounce) package tofu, firm or extra-firm

1½ tablespoons tamari or shoyu

½ teaspoon granulated garlic

⅓ cup sesame seeds (raw, untoasted)

2 teaspoons flour (whole-wheat pastry, chickpea, or brown rice)

1 tablespoon arrowroot (or cornstarch)

2 tablespoons neutral-flavored oil (sunflower, safflower, or refined coconut)

Cooking oil spray (sunflower, safflower, or refined coconut)

1. Slice the tofu into ½-inch thick slabs, and then into triangles.
2. Press the tofu by placing the pieces in a single file layer on top of paper towels (or a tea towel) then covering with additional towel(s). Press down gently, yet firmly, to remove any excess moisture.
3. Place the pressed tofu on a plate. Sprinkle evenly with the tamari and garlic. Turn to coat well.
4. In a medium bowl, combine the sesame seeds, flour, and arrowroot. Add the tofu and stir well, yet gently, with a rubber spatula so the pieces are evenly coated with the sesame mixture. Add the oil, and stir one last time to coat the tofu.
5. Spray your air fryer basket with oil. Place the tofu in a single layer in your air fryer basket and bake for 10 minutes. Remove. Turn the pieces over and cook for another 10 minutes, or until golden-brown and crisp. Remove and enjoy.

Zen Tofu

FAST / FAMILY-FRIENDLY / GLUTEN-FREE / GREEN

SERVES 3

PREP TIME:
10 MINUTES

COOK TIME:
13 MINUTES

BAKE: 374°F

Per Serving:
Calories: 96;
Total fat: 5g;
Saturated fat: 0g;
Cholesterol: 0mg;
Sodium: 343mg;
Carbohydrates: 5g;
Fiber: 2g;
Protein: 11g

This tofu might not blow your hair back, but it's actually quite lovely in its simplicity and balanced flavors. I enjoy having a low-fat, super-easy, tasty tofu recipe in my repertoire for whenever it's needed ... which is often. It's good on its own as an on-the-go high-protein snack (hello, perfect road-trip food!), or alongside some brown rice and veggies for a simple, satisfying meal. You can also add it to salads to make them a more hearty meal, or serve in sandwiches or wraps as the main filling.

1 (8-ounce) package firm
or extra-firm tofu

1 tablespoon tamari or shoyu

1 tablespoon balsamic vinegar

1 teaspoon onion granules

⅛ teaspoon turmeric powder

1 tablespoon nutritional yeast

Cooking oil spray (sunflower, safflower, or refined coconut)

1. Cut the tofu into ½-inch thick slabs and press the excess moisture out with paper towels. (To do this, lay the pieces in a single layer on paper towels—or tea towels—and cover with more towels. Press down firmly to dry the tofu slabs.)

2. Place the pressed tofu slabs on a plate and sprinkle evenly with the tamari and balsamic vinegar. Add the onion and turmeric. Turn to coat. Then sprinkle with the nutritional yeast, turning to coat again. Let sit for about 5 minutes, then turn the pieces one last time, so the tofu soaks up as much of the marinade as possible.

3. Spray an air fryer basket with oil and add the tofu pieces in a single layer. Spray the tops with oil and bake for 7 minutes. Spray the tops again, flip each piece over, and cook for another 6 minutes, or until browned and firm. Enjoy warm or cold.

Spicy Sweet Tempeh Cubes

FAST / FAMILY-FRIENDLY / GLUTEN-FREE / BLUE

SERVES 3

PREP TIME:
5 MINUTES

COOK TIME:
17 MINUTES

BAKE: 365°F

Per Serving:
Calories: 207
Total fat: 13g;
Saturated fat: 2g;
Cholesterol: 0mg;
Sodium: 679mg;
Carbohydrates: 11g;
Fiber: 0g;
Protein: 16g

This simple tempeh recipe is a staple in our house because it's versatile, tasty, and quite literally the only kind of tempeh my daughter will eat. Plus, you can feel so good about eating tempeh—it's a nutrient-dense whole food that's high in fiber, vitamins, and protein. Plus, it's been fermented, which adds another dimension of nourishment that's great for digestive health. For those who prefer milder foods, you can omit the red chili flakes, or if you adore heat, add more! These cubes can be served on salads or bowls, or as a topping for stir-fries. They're also great in wraps—my personal favorite is inside a whole-grain tortilla along with low-fat vegan mayo (or tahini), red onion, pickles, and lettuce.

8 ounces tempeh, cut into ¾-inch cubes

2 tablespoons water

2 tablespoons tamari or shoyu

1 tablespoon toasted sesame oil

2 tablespoons maple syrup

4 large garlic cloves, minced or pressed

½ teaspoon red chili flakes

1. Begin by "steaming" the tempeh, which will allow it to absorb more of the flavors: Place your tempeh cubes in a 6-inch round, 2-inch deep baking pan along with the water. Bake for 4 minutes, or until the water has evaporated. Remove the pan from the air fryer.

2. In the same pan, toss the tempeh with the tamari, sesame oil, and maple syrup. Turn well to evenly coat the tempeh cubes. If you have time, let marinate for up to 2 hours. If not, just proceed with step 3.

3. Bake the coated tempeh cubes for 4 minutes. Remove the pan from the air fryer, stir well, and bake for another 3 minutes.

4. Remove the pan and gently stir in the garlic and chili flakes. Bake for 3 minutes.

5. Remove the pan, stir, and bake for another 3 minutes, or until the marinade is absorbed and the tempeh is nicely browned. Serve hot or cold.

▶ **Air Fryer Tip:** If you're wondering why you need to use a pan for this recipe, when other recipes call for putting your food right into the basket, here's why: You don't want to lose any flavors from the marinade, or your tempeh will be rather dry and bland. Generally speaking, anytime you have a recipe with a marinade, you'll want to place it in a pan, unless all of the liquids have already been absorbed.

Cheesy Sauce

FAST / FAMILY-FRIENDLY / GLUTEN-FREE / GREEN

**MAKES
ABOUT 3 CUPS
DRY MIX**
(about
9 cups sauce)

PREP TIME:
10 MINUTES

COOK TIME:
2 TO 5 MINUTES

Per Serving
(¼ cup prepared):
Calories: 67;
Total fat: 3g;
Saturated fat: 0g;
Cholesterol: 0mg;
Sodium: 267mg;
Carbohydrates: 7g;
Fiber: 3g;
Protein: 4g

Did you ever think you'd see the day when you'd be able to enjoy a creamy, cheesy sauce that's not only vegan, but totally good for you? That day has come, and there's a 100 percent chance it'll be cheesy. This sauce boasts a high-fiber, vitamin-rich, zero-cholesterol profile, and even gives you a nice vitamin-B boost with the nutritional yeast! The addition of carrots and red peppers adds a pretty burst of color and additional nutrients. Serve over Cheesy French Fries with Shallots (page 61), BBQ Jackfruit Nachos (page 88), Mexican Stuffed Potatoes (page 92), as a dip for the Garlic Lime Tortilla Chips (page 57), or anywhere else you simply must have some additional cheesy perfection.

For the Dry Cheesy Mix

1 cup raw cashew pieces

1¼ cups nutritional yeast

½ cup rolled oats

¼ cup arrowroot (or cornstarch)

2 tablespoons seasoned salt

2 tablespoons garlic granules

1½ tablespoons onion granules

½ teaspoon ground turmeric

For the Cheesy Sauce (makes 3 cups)

1 cup Dry Cheesy Mix

¼ cup grated carrots

¼ cup roasted red peppers
(the jarred variety is fine)

2 cups water, divided

To make the Dry Cheesy Mix

In a food processor, place the cashews, nutritional yeast, oats, arrowroot, salt, garlic and onion granules, and turmeric. Blend into a fine powder. At this point, this dry mix will store in the fridge (in an airtight container) for months.

To make the Cheesy Sauce

1. In a blender jar, add the Dry Cheesy Mix, carrots, red pepper, and 1 cup water and blend until as smooth as possible. Add the remaining 1 cup water and blend well, until very smooth.
2. To thicken, place in a small pot over medium heat. Cook, whisking very often, until thickened (this should take less than 2 minutes). Serve warm.

▶ **Cooking Tip:** This recipe has been formulated so that you can make up a large quantity of the Dry Cheesy Mix and keep it on hand in the fridge—which will shortcut your future cheesy escapades. Once you have the dry mix made up, it takes less than 5 minutes to transform it into velvety, warm cheese sauce. I also like to do the following to create a second shortcut: When I know I'll be using lots of cheesy sauce for the week, I'll blend up the dry mix, carrots, red pepper, and water. From there, this liquid mixture will keep in the fridge for up to one week, and then it only takes a minute to whisk it into a thick sauce on the stove— perfect for busy nights!

Asian Spicy Sweet Sauce

FAST / FAMILY-FRIENDLY / GLUTEN-FREE / BLUE

MAKES ABOUT 1 CUP

PREP TIME:
5 MINUTES

COOK TIME:
3 TO 5 MINUTES

Per Serving
(2 tablespoons):
Calories: 80;
Total fat: 2g;
Saturated fat: 0g;
Cholesterol: 0mg;
Sodium: 0mg;
Carbohydrates: 17g;
Fiber: 1g;
Protein: 0g

This is a delicious, easy-to-prepare sauce that goes well with the Air-Fried Spring Rolls (page 70), Crisp Tofu (page 132), and the Asian Buffet Bowl (page 99). It's also a great component to have on hand when you want to jazz up steamed vegetables, brown rice, tempeh, or tofu. For those who prefer milder foods, you can also omit the red chili flakes—or if you're a heat-lover like me, add more! Be sure to use toasted sesame oil here (it's dark in color and available in grocery stores, health food stores, and Asian markets), as there's just no replacement for aromatic, flavorful toasted sesame.

2 teaspoons arrowroot (or cornstarch)

½ cup water, divided

¼ cup tamari or shoyu

¼ cup agave nectar

1 tablespoon toasted sesame oil

4 large garlic cloves, minced or pressed

¼ to ½ teaspoon red chili flakes (adjust according to your heat preference)

1. In a medium pan, whisk the arrowroot with 1 tablespoon of the water until dissolved.
2. Add the remaining water, tamari, agave, sesame oil, garlic, and chili flakes and whisk over medium heat. Continue to cook, whisking often, until it becomes thicker in consistency.
3. Remove from heat when lightly thickened. This will keep, refrigerated in an airtight container, for at least 2 weeks.

No-Dairy Ranch Dressing

FAST / FAMILY-FRIENDLY / GLUTEN-FREE / BLUE

**MAKES
8 SERVINGS**
(about 1 cup)

PREP TIME:
5 MINUTES

Per Serving:
Calories: 76;
Total fat: 7g;
Saturated fat: 0g;
Cholesterol: 0mg;
Sodium: 258mg;
Carbohydrates: 3g;
Fiber: 0g;
Protein: 1g

The wonderful thing about a good vegan ranch is that just about everyone will love it, whether they're a picky omnivore or a dedicated vegan. I've served this to countless omnivores (many of them unsuspecting kids), and they've all said they wouldn't have known it was vegan—which is definitely a plus if you've got skeptics to feed! You can greatly vary the consistency and flavor of your ranch dressing by finding a vegan mayonnaise that you love. Personally, I prefer reduced-fat Vegenaise brand, because it's made with healthier oils (and I like the taste just as much as full-fat varieties). However, you're welcome to use any kind you like, as most varieties of vegan mayo will work well. This dressing is great over salads and potatoes, or as a dip for the Low-Fat, High-Flavor Buffalo Cauliflower (page 50) and Crunchy Onion Rings (page 52). If you have a big family (or just eat unusual amounts of ranch dressing), you may wish to double this recipe.

1 cup prepared vegan mayonnaise, your choice

4 teaspoons apple cider vinegar

4 teaspoons minced fresh parsley (or 1 tablespoon dried parsley)

4 small to medium garlic cloves, pressed or finely minced

1 teaspoon onion granules

½ teaspoon sea salt

In a jar, add the mayonnaise, vinegar, parsley, garlic, onion, and salt, cover tightly, and shake well until thoroughly combined. Alternatively, you can stir the ingredients together in a bowl if you're feeling extra civilized.

▶ **Cooking Tip:** If your dressing is too thick, add up to 2 tablespoons water until your desired consistency is reached. (I've found that this really depends on the type of vegan mayo you use.) This will keep, refrigerated in an airtight container, for a week or more.

Green Chili Sauce

FAST / GLUTEN-FREE / GREEN

**MAKES
ABOUT 2 CUPS**

PREP TIME:
5 MINUTES

COOK TIME:
5 MINUTES

Per Serving
(¼ cup) :
Calories: 21;
Total fat: 1g;
Saturated fat: 0g;
Cholesterol: 0mg;
Sodium: 76mg;
Carbohydrates: 4g;
Fiber: 0g;
Protein: 1g

This fabulous flavor explosion is the perfect complement to Potato Flautas with Green Chili Sauce (page 30), tamales, air-fried 10-Minute Chimichanga (page 90), burritos, tacos, tostadas, potatoes, and beans. This sauce is one of my absolute faves, because it's mouthwateringly delicious, yet immune-boosting and chock-full of superfoods. It's high in vitamin C (from the green chiles), and the fresh garlic and lime juice are perfect for kicking out a cold! You can find roasted, chopped chiles in the frozen Mexican or vegetable section of most supermarkets. When in season, you can find green chiles at your local farmers' market—as well as most supermarkets, and you can easily roast them in your air fryer!

1 teaspoon neutral-flavored oil (sunflower, safflower, or refined coconut)

1 tablespoon flour (brown rice or chickpea)

1 (13-ounce) container (about 1½ cups) roasted, peeled, chopped green chiles, thawed if frozen

2 teaspoons coconut sugar

¼ cup plus 1 teaspoon fresh lime juice

1¼ teaspoons sea salt

5 medium garlic cloves, minced or pressed

1. In a medium saucepan, add the oil and flour and stir until smooth. Add the green chiles and coconut sugar, and cook over medium-high heat for about 5 minutes, stirring often, until a bit thicker in consistency.

2. Turn off the heat and stir in the lime juice, sea salt, and garlic. Combine well and serve. This will store, refrigerated in an airtight container, for about a week.

▶ **Cooking Tip:** If you prefer a very thick sauce, you may add a little more flour until the desired consistency is reached. You may also wish to use mild (vs. medium or hot) green chiles, even if you like spicy foods. I've found that even mild green chiles are often fairly spicy, and if you're like me and want to eat a little too much of this sauce at a time, you may not want the heat to be overwhelming.

Cilantro Chutney

FAST / GLUTEN-FREE / GREEN

**MAKES ABOUT
1½ CUPS**

PREP TIME:
10 MINUTES

Per Serving
(2 tablespoons) :
Calories: 21;
Total fat: 2g;
Saturated fat: 1g;
Cholesterol: 0mg;
Sodium: 80mg;
Carbohydrates: 2g;
Fiber: 1g;
Protein: 0g

If you adore Indian food (even half as much as I do), this chutney will become a favorite addition to your regular recipe rotation. Not only is it flavorful, it's also totally good for you, due to the iron-rich, detoxifying cilantro, immune-boosting garlic, and all-around nourishing magic of ginger. This delightfully fresh-tasting dip is the perfect complement to Gluten-Free "Samosas" (page 64), Save-Some-For-Me Pakoras (page 68), and the Crispy Indian Wrap (page 75). You can also use it as a seriously fun alternative to ketchup for the Classic French Fries (page 60) or Crunchy Onion Rings (page 52). Or just eat it with a spoon, as I clearly would.

1 cup fresh cilantro

⅓ cup finely shredded unsweetened coconut

2 tablespoons chopped fresh ginger

3 medium garlic cloves, peeled

½ jalapeño, seeds removed

1 teaspoon cumin seeds

½ teaspoon sea salt

2 tablespoons fresh lime juice

½ cup water

1. In a food processor or blender, place the cilantro, coconut, ginger, garlic, and jalapeño. Blend thoroughly, although the mixture shouldn't be totally smooth.

2. Add the cumin, salt, lime juice, and water and blend until thoroughly combined, but with a tiny bit of texture still remaining. Serve cold or at room temperature. This will keep in the fridge for 1 or 2 weeks when stored in an airtight container.

AIR FRYER VEGAN FOOD CHART

FRESH FRUIT	QUANTITY	TIME	TEMP	NOTES
Apples	1 to 3 cups	4 to 7 minutes	350°F	Cut first. Sprinkle with cinnamon and nutmeg.
Bananas	1 to 3 cups	4 to 7 minutes	350°F	Peel and slice.
Peaches	1 to 3 cups	5 to 6 minutes	350°F	Cut first. Sprinkle lightly with fresh thyme if desired.

FRESH VEGETABLES	QUANTITY	TIME	TEMP	NOTES
Asparagus	½ pound	5 to 8 minutes	400°F	Trim ends, spray with oil, and sprinkle with seasonings.
Broccoli	1 to 2 cups	5 to 8 minutes	400°F	Spray with olive oil, and sprinkle with seasonings.
Brussels sprouts	1 cup	13 to 15 minutes	380°F	Trim bottoms and cut in half, spray with olive oil, and sprinkle with seasonings.
Carrots	½ to 1 cup	7 to 10 minutes	380°F	Cut, spray with oil, and sprinkle with seasonings.
Cauliflower florets	1 to 2 cups	9 to 10 minutes	360°F	Spray with olive oil, and sprinkle with seasonings.
Corn on the cob	2 ears	6 minutes	390°F	Spray with oil, and sprinkle with seasonings.
Eggplant	½ to 2 pounds	13 to 15 minutes	400°F	Cut into thin slices, marinate, spray with olive oil, and flip halfway through cooking.
Green beans	½ to 1 pound	5 minutes	400°F	Trim ends, spray with olive oil, and shake halfway through cooking.
Kale	½ bunch	10 to 12 minutes	275°F	Trim leaves from ribs, and season with oil, vinegar, and seasonings.

FRESH VEGETABLES	QUANTITY	TIME	TEMP	NOTES
Mushrooms	½ to 1 cup	5 to 8 minutes	400°F	Trim stems, and sprinkle with seasonings or coat with a breading.
Onions	½ to 1 pound	5 to 8 minutes	370°F	Slice, spray with oil, and sprinkle with salt.
Peppers (bell)	½ to 1 cup	6 to 8 minutes	370°F	Cut, spray with oil, and toss with seasonings.
Potatoes (baked)	1 to 2 pounds	40 minutes	400°F	Poke holes first, spray with olive oil, and cook.
Potatoes (cubed)	1 to 2 cups	15 minutes	400°F	Spray with olive oil, season, and shake halfway through cooking.
Potatoes (fries)	1 to 2 cups	15 minutes	380°F	Spray cut potatoes with olive oil, sprinkle with seasonings, and shake halfway through cooking.
Potatoes (wedges)	1 to 3 cups	18 to 20 minutes	380°F	Spray with olive oil, season, and shake halfway through cooking.
Squash	½ pound	12 to 13 minutes	400°F	Spray with oil, and sprinkle with salt, coconut sugar, and rosemary.
Sweet potatoes (baked)	1 large or 2 small sweet potatoes	35 to 40 minutes	390°F	Poke holes first, spray with oil, and cook.
Sweet potatoes (cubed)	1 to 3 cups	14 to 20 minutes	380°F	Spray with oil, and shake halfway through cooking.
Sweet potatoes (fries)	1 to 2 cups	25 minutes	380°F	Spray with oil, sprinkle with rosemary and salt, and shake halfway through cooking.
Tomatoes (breaded)	1 to 2 tomatoes	10 minutes	350°F	Cut in half, season or bread, and spray with olive oil.
Zucchini	½ to 1 pound	10 to 12 minutes	370°F	Cut first, spray with oil, and sprinkle with seasonings.

THE DIRTY DOZEN AND THE CLEAN FIFTEEN™

A nonprofit environmental watchdog organization called Environmental Working Group (EWG) looks at data supplied by the United States Department of Agriculture (USDA) and the Food and Drug Administration (FDA) about pesticide residues. Each year it compiles a list of the best and worst pesticide loads found in commercial crops. You can use these lists to decide which fruits and vegetables to buy organic to minimize your exposure to pesticides and which produce is considered safe enough to buy conventionally. This does not mean they are pesticide-free, though, so wash these fruits and vegetables thoroughly. The list is updated annually, and you can find it online at EWG.org/FoodNews.

Dirty Dozen™

1. strawberries
2. spinach
3. kale
4. nectarines
5. apples
6. grapes
7. peaches
8. cherries
9. pears
10. tomatoes
11. celery
12. potatoes

†Additionally, nearly three-quarters of hot pepper samples contained pesticide residues.

Clean Fifteen™

1. avocados
2. sweet corn
3. pineapples
4. sweet peas (frozen)
5. onions
6. papayas
7. eggplants
8. asparagus
9. kiwis
10. cabbages
11. cauliflower
12. cantaloupes
13. broccoli
14. mushrooms
15. honeydew melons

MEASUREMENT CONVERSIONS

VOLUME EQUIVALENTS (LIQUID)

US STANDARD	US STANDARD (OUNCES)	METRIC (APPROX.)
2 tablespoons	1 fl. oz.	30 mL
¼ cup	2 fl. oz.	60 mL
½ cup	4 fl. oz.	120 mL
1 cup	8 fl. oz.	240 mL
1½ cups	12 fl. oz.	355 mL
2 cups or 1 pint	16 fl. oz.	475 mL
4 cups or 1 quart	32 fl. oz.	1 L
1 gallon	128 fl. oz.	4 L

OVEN TEMPERATURES

FAHRENHEIT (F)	CELSIUS (C) (APPROX.)
250°F	120°C
300°F	150°C
325°F	165°C
350°F	180°C
375°F	190°C
400°F	200°C
425°F	220°C
450°F	230°C

VOLUME EQUIVALENTS (DRY)

US STANDARD	METRIC (APPROX.)
⅛ teaspoon	0.5 mL
¼ teaspoon	1 mL
½ teaspoon	2 mL
¾ teaspoon	4 mL
1 teaspoon	5 mL
1 tablespoon	15 mL
¼ cup	59 mL
⅓ cup	79 mL
½ cup	118 mL
⅔ cup	156 mL
¾ cup	177 mL
1 cup	235 mL
2 cups or 1 pint	475 mL
3 cups	700 mL
4 cups or 1 quart	1 L

WEIGHT EQUIVALENTS

US STANDARD (OUNCES)	METRIC (APPROX.)
½ ounce	15 g
1 ounce	30 g
2 ounces	60 g
4 ounces	115 g
8 ounces	225 g
12 ounces	340 g
16 ounces or 1 pound	455 g

RECOMMENDATIONS AND RESOURCES

Books

New Whole Foods Encyclopedia **(Rebecca Wood):** This well-written book contains a wealth of information on plant-based foods (although it's not a strictly vegan book).

The Vegan Air Fryer **(JL Fields):** Even more great air fryer recipes for your repertoire!

NYC Vegan **(Michael Suchman and Ethan Ciment):** My daughter has two books she loves to cook from—*Radiant Health, Inner Wealth* (my first cookbook), and this! She says the crepe recipe in this book is the cat's meow.

Radiant Health, Inner Wealth, The Two-Week Wellness Solution, Radiance 4 Life, 100 Vegan Entrées, and FOOD LOVE: These are resources I've made available on my own website, www.tesschallis.com.

Gluten-Free Resources

Julie Hasson: This lovely lady is a genius when it comes to vegan, gluten-free breads. Find great recipes on www.julieandkittee.com.

Kim and Jake's: Their gluten-free bread, buns, and rolls are absolutely delicious—and made with heathier ingredients than your typical GF breads. I actually use my air fryer to heat up their rolls!

Jovial brand pasta (organic brown rice pasta): I've found this is the absolute best gluten-free pasta, as it cooks up perfectly every time (never mushy, unlike many other GF pastas) and has a wonderful texture and neutral, pleasant flavor.

My Ten Favorite Food Spots in the U.S.

1. **Watercourse** (Denver, CO): When I'm in Denver, I eat at this fabulous all-vegan spot almost daily.

2. **Oryana Community Co-Op** (Traverse City, MI): I heart this place hard-core. When I'm in Michigan in the summer, I eat almost all my meals here, because it's almost like eating at home.

3. **Seabirds Kitchen** (Long Beach, CA): This all-vegan spot is spot-on with their full-flavored menu!

4. **Ruchi** (Chandler, AZ): This vegetarian Indian place is one of my daughter's favorites. Raj, the owner, treats us like family, and almost everything on the menu can be made vegan. Oh, and their lunch buffet is unreal!

5. **Shizen Vegan Sushi Bar** (San Francisco, CA): Their creative vegan sushi is next level! A treat for all the senses.

6. **Ionie Raw Food Café** (Sarasota, FL): I have a special place in my heart for Ionie and her magical little café! The raw vegan food there is some of the best I've ever had.

7. **Casa Terra** (Glendale, AZ): It's so wonderful to have a fine dining spot near Phoenix that's all vegan and so fresh and elegant.

8. **Inn Season Café** (Royal Oak, MI): My friend Lisa and I have made a tradition of going to this wonderful little spot for brunch when I visit each summer. Their unpretentious food is so fresh, nourishing, and flavorful.

9. **Violette's Vegan** (Las Vegas, NV): I was impressed by the tasty, full-flavored food and warm service at this all-vegan spot—their zucchini sticks had me at hello.

10. **Local Juicery** (Flagstaff, AZ): This high-vibe spot has an all-organic, plant-based menu and really knows how to make healthy food taste delicious! They also have a second location in Sedona.

A

Air fryers, 1–15
advantages of, 2
buying, 3–4
cleaning, 6
cooking times and tempera-
tures for, 6
food chart for, 144–45
frequently asked questions
about, 7
how they work, 3
step-by-step instructions for, 5
tips for, 6
types of foods and, 9
Apples, 144
Apple Cobbler Oatmeal, 19
Apple Puffs with Vanilla Caramel
Sauce, 118–19
Cozy Apple Crisp, 116–17
De-Light-Full Caramelized
Apples, 115
Arrowroot, 10
Asparagus, 144
Avocado
Potato Flautas with Green Chili
Sauce, 30–31
Roasted Vegetable Tacos, 32–33

B

Baking-specific staples, 10
Balsamic Glazed Carrots, 47
Bananas, 144
Banana Chia Bread, 26
Banana Churro Oatmeal, 24–25
Beans
Crispy Indian Wrap, 75–76
green beans, 144
Kids' Taquitos, 94
Mexican Stuffed Potatoes, 92–93
Mung Bean "Quiche" with Lime
Garlic Sauce, 40–41
Our Daily Bean, 86
Roasted Vegetable Tacos, 32–33
Taco Salad with Creamy Lime
Sauce, 87
Tamale Pie with Cilantro Lime
Cornmeal Crust, 96–97

10-Minute Chimichanga, 90–91
Berbere-Spiced Fries, 62
Berries
Blackberry Peach Cobbler, 128–29
Blueberry Breakfast Cobbler, 18
Raspberry Lemon Streusel
Cake, 124–25
Strawberry Delight Breakfast
Parfait, 21
Strawberry Puffs with Creamy
Lemon Sauce, 120–21
Blackberry Peach Cobbler, 128–29
Blueberry Breakfast Cobbler, 18
Breads
Banana Chia Bread, 26
Delish Donut Holes, 22–23
Whole-Grain Corn Bread, 27
Breakfast
Apple Cobbler Oatmeal, 19
Banana Churro Oatmeal, 24–25
Blueberry Breakfast Cobbler, 18
Cheesy Pleasy Breakfast Sand-
wich, 38–39
Delish Donut Holes, 22–23
Garlic Rosemary Home Fries, 37
Gorgeous Granola, 20
Hearty Breakfast Burrito, 34–35
Mung Bean "Quiche" with Lime
Garlic Sauce, 40–41
Noochy Tofu, 36
Potato Flautas with Green Chili
Sauce, 30–31
Roasted Vegetable Tacos, 32–33
Smart & Savory Breakfast
Cakes, 28–29
Strawberry Delight Breakfast
Parfait, 21
Broccoli, 144
Everyday Power Noodles, 104–5
Hearty Breakfast Burrito, 34–35
Brussels sprouts, 144
Sweet Miso-Glazed Brussels
Sprouts, 63

C

Cabbage
Air-Fried Spring Rolls, 70–71

Crispy Indian Wrap, 75–76
Everyday Power Noodles, 104–5
Ginger Tahini Noodles with
Sesame Crunch Tofu, 98
Taco Salad with Creamy Lime
Sauce, 87
Cakes
"How Is This Vegan?" Chocolate
Cake, 108–9
Pineapple Upside-Down
Cake, 126–27
Raspberry Lemon Streusel
Cake, 124–25
Carrots, 144
Air-Fried Spring Rolls, 70–71
Balsamic Glazed Carrots, 47
Cauliflower, 144
Low-Fat, High-Flavor Buffalo
Cauliflower, 50–51
Pasta with Creamy Cauliflower
Sauce, 82–83
Cheese, vegan
Easy Peasy Pizza, 77
Immune-Boosting Grilled Cheese
Sandwich, 95
Kids' Taquitos, 94
Cheesy Sauce, 138–39
BBQ Jackfruit Nachos, 88–89
Cheesy French Fries with
Shallots, 61
Cheesy Pleasy Breakfast
Sandwich, 38–39
Easy Peasy Pizza, 77
Mexican Stuffed Potatoes, 92–93
Chia seeds
Banana Chia Bread, 26
Chickpea flour (garbanzo bean
flour), 9
Eggplant Parmigiana, 78–79
Save-Some-For-Me Pakoras, 68–69
Smart & Savory Breakfast
Cakes, 28–29
Chiles
Green Chili Sauce, 142
Potato Flautas with Green Chili
Sauce, 30–31
Chocolate

Chocolate Chip Cookies, 110–11
"How Is This Vegan?" Chocolate
    Cake, 108–9
Cilantro
    Cilantro Chutney, 143
    Crispy Indian Wrap, 75–76
    Ginger Tahini Noodles with
        Sesame Crunch Tofu, 98
    Gluten-Free "Samosas" with
        Cilantro Chutney, 64–65
    Save-Some-For-Me Pakoras,
        68–69
    Taco Salad with Creamy Lime
        Sauce, 87
    Tamale Pie with Cilantro Lime
        Cornmeal Crust, 96–97
Cinnamon
    Cozy Apple Crisp, 116–17
    Easy Cinnamon Crisps, 114
Cobblers
    Apple Cobbler Oatmeal, 19
    Blackberry Peach Cobbler,
        128–29
    Blueberry Breakfast Cobbler, 18
Cookies
    Chocolate Chip Cookies, 110–11
    Oatmeal Raisin Cookies,
        112–13
Cornmeal
    (Air) Fried Green
        Tomatoes, 48–49
    Tamale Pie with Cilantro Lime
        Cornmeal Crust, 96–97
    Whole-Grain Corn Bread, 27
Corn on the cob, 144
Cucumber
    Ginger Tahini Noodles with
        Sesame Crunch Tofu, 98

D
Desserts
    Apple Puffs with Vanilla Caramel
        Sauce, 118–19
    Blackberry Peach Cobbler,
        128–29
    Chocolate Chip Cookies, 110–11
    Cozy Apple Crisp, 116–17
    De-Light-Full Caramelized
        Apples, 115
    Easy Cinnamon Crisps, 114
    Gooey Lemon Bars, 122–23

"How Is This Vegan?" Chocolate
    Cake, 108–9
Oatmeal Raisin Cookies, 112–13
Pineapple Upside-Down
    Cake, 126–27
Raspberry Lemon Streusel
    Cake, 124–25
Strawberry Puffs with Creamy
    Lemon Sauce, 120–21
Dirty Dozen and Clean
    Fifteen, 146
Dressing
    No-Dairy Ranch Dressing, 141

E
Eggplant, 144
    Eggplant Parmigiana, 78–79
    Tamari Roasted Eggplant, 46

F
Favorite food spots in the U.S., 149
Flaxseed, ground (flaxmeal), 10
    Banana Chia Bread, 26
Food chart, 144–45
Fruit. See also specific
    Dirty Dozen and Clean
        Fifteen, 146
    in food chart, 144

G
Garbanzo bean flour. See
    Chickpea flour
Garlic
    Air-Fried Spring Rolls, 70–71
    Garlic Lime Tortilla Chips, 57
    Garlic Rosemary Home
        Fries, 37
    Mung Bean "Quiche" with Lime
        Garlic Sauce, 40–41
    Ginger Tahini Noodles with
        Sesame Crunch Tofu, 98
Granola
    Apple Cobbler Oatmeal, 19
    Blueberry Breakfast Cobbler, 18
    Gorgeous Granola, 20
    Strawberry Delight Breakfast
        Parfait, 21
Green beans, 144

J
Jackfruit
    BBQ Jackfruit Nachos, 88–89

K
Kale, 144
    Alethea's Kale Chips, 55
    Smart & Savory Breakfast
        Cakes, 28–29

L
Lemon
    Gooey Lemon Bars, 122–23
    Lemony Lentils with "Fried"
        Onions, 84–85
    Raspberry Lemon Streusel
        Cake, 124–25
    Strawberry Puffs with Creamy
        Lemon Sauce, 120–21
Lentils
    Lemony Lentils with "Fried"
        Onions, 84–85
Lettuce
    Taco Salad with Creamy Lime
        Sauce, 87
    10-Minute Chimichanga, 90–91
Lime
    Garlic Lime Tortilla Chips, 57
    Mung Bean "Quiche" with Lime
        Garlic Sauce, 40–41
    Roasted Shishito Peppers with
        Lime, 54
    Taco Salad with Creamy Lime
        Sauce, 87
    Tamale Pie with Cilantro Lime
        Cornmeal Crust, 96–97

M
Main dishes
    Asian Buffet Bowl with Crisp
        Tofu, 99
    BBQ Jackfruit Nachos, 88–89
    Crispy Indian Wrap, 75–76
    Crispy Salt and Pepper Tofu, 74
    Easy Peasy Pizza, 77
    Eggplant Parmigiana, 78–79
    Everyday Power Noodles, 104–5
    Ginger Tahini Noodles with
        Sesame Crunch Tofu, 98
    Immune-Boosting Grilled Cheese
        Sandwich, 95
    Kids' Taquitos, 94
    Lemony Lentils with "Fried"
        Onions, 84–85
    Luscious Lazy Lasagna, 80–81

Mexican Stuffed Potatoes, 92–93
Our Daily Bean, 86
Panang Curry Bowl, 100–101
Pasta with Creamy Cauliflower Sauce, 82–83
Red Curry Noodles with Sesame Crunch Tofu, 102–3
Taco Salad with Creamy Lime Sauce, 87
Tamale Pie with Cilantro Lime Cornmeal Crust, 96–97
10-Minute Chimichanga, 90–91
Mayonnaise
No-Dairy Ranch Dressing, 141
Meal preparation, 12
Measurement conversions, 147
Miso
Everyday Power Noodles, 104–5
Sweet Miso-Glazed Brussels Sprouts, 63
Mung Bean "Quiche" with Lime Garlic Sauce, 40–41
Mushrooms, 145
Air-Fried Spring Rolls, 70–71
Everyday Power Noodles, 104–5

N

Noodles
Asian Buffet Bowl with Crisp Tofu, 99
Everyday Power Noodles, 104–5
Ginger Tahini Noodles with Sesame Crunch Tofu, 98
Panang Curry Bowl, 100–101
Red Curry Noodles with Sesame Crunch Tofu, 102–3
Nutritional yeast, 10

O

Oats, 10
Apple Cobbler Oatmeal, 19
Banana Churro Oatmeal, 24–25
Blackberry Peach Cobbler, 128–29
Gorgeous Granola, 20
Oatmeal Raisin Cookies, 112–13
Oil, 3, 10, 13
Oil spray, 6, 10
Okra
Indian Spiced Okra, 66–67

Onions, 145
Crunchy Onion Rings, 52–53
Lemony Lentils with "Fried" Onions, 84–85
Save-Some-For-Me Pakoras, 68–69

P

Pantry staples, 9–10
Pasta
Luscious Lazy Lasagna, 80–81
Pasta with Creamy Cauliflower Sauce, 82–83
Peaches, 144
Blackberry Peach Cobbler, 128–29
Peppers, bell, 145
Hearty Breakfast Burrito, 34–35
Peppers, chili. See Chiles
Peppers, shishito
Roasted Shishito Peppers with Lime, 54
Phyllo dough
Apple Puffs with Vanilla Caramel Sauce, 118–19
Strawberry Puffs with Creamy Lemon Sauce, 120–21
Pineapple Upside-Down Cake, 126–27
Plant-based milk, 10
Potatoes, 145
Berbere-Spiced Fries, 62
Classic French Fries, 60
Crispy Indian Wrap, 75–76
Garlic Rosemary Home Fries, 37
Gluten-Free "Samosas" with Cilantro Chutney, 64–65
Hearty Breakfast Burrito, 34–35
Mexican Stuffed Potatoes, 92–93
Potato Flautas with Green Chili Sauce, 30–31
Smart & Savory Breakfast Cakes, 28–29

R

Raisins
Oatmeal Raisin Cookies, 112–13
Raspberry Lemon Streusel Cake, 124–25
Recipe guide, 14–15
Recommendations and resources, 148–149

Rice
Asian Buffet Bowl with Crisp Tofu, 99
Panang Curry Bowl, 100–101
Rice paper wrappers
Air-Fried Spring Rolls, 70–71
Gluten-Free "Samosas" with Cilantro Chutney, 64–65
Rosemary
Garlic Rosemary Home Fries, 37
Rosemary Sweet Potato Chips, 58–59

S

Salad
Taco Salad with Creamy Lime Sauce, 87
Salad dressing
No-Dairy Ranch Dressing, 141
Sauces
Asian Spicy Sweet Sauce, 140
Cheesy Sauce, 138–39
Green Chili Sauce, 142
No-Dairy Ranch Dressing, 141
Scallions
Everyday Power Noodles, 104–5
Sesame
Ginger Tahini Noodles with Sesame Crunch Tofu, 98
Red Curry Noodles with Sesame Crunch Tofu, 102–3
Sesame Crunch Tofu, 134
Shallots
Cheesy French Fries with Shallots, 61
Shopping, 12
Shoyu, 10
Side dishes and snacks
Addictive Zucchini Sticks, 44
(Air) Fried Green Tomatoes, 48–49
Air-Fried Spring Rolls, 70–71
Alethea's Kale Chips, 55
Balsamic Glazed Carrots, 47
Berbere-Spiced Fries, 62
Cheesy French Fries with Shallots, 61
Classic French Fries, 60

Crunchy Onion Rings, 52–53
Garlic Lime Tortilla Chips, 57
Gluten-Free "Samosas" with
    Cilantro Chutney, 64–65
Indian Spiced Okra, 66–67
Low-Fat, High-Flavor Buffalo
    Cauliflower, 50–51
Roasted Shishito Peppers with
    Lime, 54
Rosemary Sweet Potato
    Chips, 58–59
Save-Some-For-Me Pakoras, 68–69
Simple Roasted Zucchini, 45
Sweet Miso-Glazed Brussels
    Sprouts, 63
Tamari Roasted Eggplant, 46
Timeless Taro Chips, 56
Spice rack staples, 11
Spinach
    Luscious Lazy Lasagna, 80–81
Squash, 145
Staples
    Asian Spicy Sweet Sauce, 140
    Cheesy Sauce, 138–39
    Cilantro Chutney, 143
    Crisp Tofu, 132–33
    Green Chili Sauce, 142
    No-Dairy Ranch Dressing, 141
    Sesame Crunch Tofu, 134
    Spicy Sweet Tempeh
        Cubes, 136–37
    Zen Tofu, 135
Strawberries
    Strawberry Delight Breakfast
        Parfait, 21
    Strawberry Puffs with Creamy
        Lemon Sauce, 120–21
Sweet potatoes, 145
    Rosemary Sweet Potato
        Chips, 58–59

T

Tahini
    Ginger Tahini Noodles with
        Sesame Crunch Tofu, 98
Tamari, 10
    Tamari Roasted Eggplant, 46
Taro
    Timeless Taro Chips, 56
Tempeh
    Spicy Sweet Tempeh
        Cubes, 136–37
Tofu, 133
    Asian Buffet Bowl with Crisp
        Tofu, 99
    Cheesy Pleasy Breakfast
        Sandwich, 38–39
    Crisp Tofu, 132–33
    Crispy Salt and Pepper Tofu, 74
    Everyday Power Noodles, 104–5
    Ginger Tahini Noodles with
        Sesame Crunch Tofu, 98
    Hearty Breakfast Burrito, 34–35
    Luscious Lazy Lasagna, 80–81
    Noochy Tofu, 36
    Panang Curry Bowl, 100–101
    Red Curry Noodles with Sesame
        Crunch Tofu, 102–3
    Sesame Crunch Tofu, 134
    Strawberry Delight Breakfast
        Parfait, 21
    Taco Salad with Creamy Lime
        Sauce, 87
    Zen Tofu, 135
Tomatoes, 145
    (Air) Fried Green
        Tomatoes, 48–49
    BBQ Jackfruit Nachos, 88–89
    Mexican Stuffed Potatoes, 92–93
    Taco Salad with Creamy Lime
        Sauce, 87

Tamale Pie with Cilantro Lime
    Cornmeal Crust, 96–97
Tortillas
    BBQ Jackfruit Nachos, 88–89
    Crispy Indian Wrap, 75–76
    Easy Cinnamon Crisps, 114
    Easy Peasy Pizza, 77
    Garlic Lime Tortilla Chips, 57
    Hearty Breakfast Burrito, 34–35
    Kids' Taquitos, 94
    Potato Flautas with Green Chili
        Sauce, 30–31
    Roasted Vegetable Tacos, 32–33
    10-Minute Chimichanga, 90–91

V

Vanilla bean
    Apple Puffs with Vanilla Caramel
        Sauce, 118–19
Vegetables. See also specific
    Dirty Dozen and Clean
        Fifteen, 146
    in food chart, 144–45

W

Whole-wheat pastry flour, 10

Y

Yeast, nutritional, 10

Z

Zucchini, 145
    Addictive Zucchini Sticks, 44
    Roasted Vegetable Tacos, 32–33
    Simple Roasted Zucchini, 45
    Tamale Pie with Cilantro Lime
        Cornmeal Crust, 96–97

ACKNOWLEDGMENTS

So much to be grateful for!

First of all, thanks to the great team at Callisto—Bridget, you made the editing process fun and joyful, which is pretty amazing!

I also owe a debt of gratitude to my recipe testers—you are responsible for my face smiling at the computer screen way more than you could ever know! Your feedback made this book better, and the process so much more fun. Thanks so much, Kathleen Evey-Walters, Kathy Bethune, Luba Hoffman, Sherrie Thompson, Sharon Carr, Anastacia Norris, Christian Shepard, Sue O'Halleran, Isabel Rivas-Vita, Kassidy Bennett, Ingrid Gold, Leslie Finnegan Conn, Melody Hodges, Melissa Ruggiano, Michelle Wilson, Tammy Primack-Bedard, Jenni Petite Fleur, Nicole Lueders, Mikayla Erickson, Duann Ashcraft, Tianna Lee, Linzey Seiber, Jan Cawthorne, Patty Femminella Stein, and Carissa Danielle! Y'all are rock stars.

Luckily, my cousin and soul sis Stacia was around during the early stages of recipe testing, and had some wonderful ideas that really enriched some of these recipes—thank you, lady! And John Perkins, it was way too much fun cooking these recipes for you—your palate is perfection, as is your heart.

Last but never least, I'm thankful to my beautiful daughter, Alethea, who brings me joy and laughter every day—and who was the inspiration for so much of this book.

I love and appreciate you all!

Tess Challis is the author of six cookbooks, a speaker, and a "One Degree" life coach.

After going vegan in 1991, she felt compelled (and slightly desperate) to learn how to cook. Eventually, she developed a knack for creating full-flavored vegan dishes and began teaching cooking classes. This led to work as a personal chef, caterer, and author; as well as developing recipes for food lines and presenting vegan cooking demonstrations across the country. Over the years, she's also had a bit too much fun helping people make their transition to veganism a joyful, low-stress one by showing them how to shop, cook, plan, and make their kitchen an organized, healthy, happy place.

Tess has overcome a plethora of challenges, including obesity, anxiety, depression, severe acne, and chronic illness. She loves showing people the level of change that's possible when you combine inner wellness practices with healthy plant-based eating.

She currently resides in Chandler, Arizona, with her daughter, Alethea. Visit TessChallis.com for recipes, information, and inspiration.

Printed in the USA
CPSIA information can be obtained
at www.ICGtesting.com
CBHW040709270224
4689CB00002B/5